Praise for *Alfredo's Journey*

"As a clinician and academic, one can study and research every known aspect of a disorder and write scholarly articles for learned journals, but none of this holds the potency of an individual relaying his or her lived experience. Alfredo does just this in his inimitable style offering hope at every juncture to those who travel a similar road. The story should be read by clinicians, academics and sufferers alike."

Professor Trevor Waring AM,
Clinical Psychologist
Con-Joint Professor of Psychology, University of Newcastle

"Alfredo's story and his insights into the causes and treatment of mental ill-health are incredibly moving and impressive. His humanity, intelligence, creativity (in multiple domains of art, music, writing and scholarship) and his generosity and compassion, including towards people affected by mental illness and in a touching fashion to dedicated mental health professionals, shine through the pages of his book. He also reveals a capacity for forgiveness towards his own family. There are many memorable passages, but my favourite is to be found in Chapter 5, in which Alfredo describes how he helped Boris, a fellow hospital patient, to trust him and to withstand the fury of psychotic experiences preventing any recourse to extra medication or restraint. The book is a complex mixture of autobiography, analysis, teaching and inspiration. Alfredo illustrates the interaction between the hidden vulnerability for mental ill health we all face, our early and indeed later life experiences, especially trauma and loss, and the healing force of other human beings and a caring society and genuine expertise in mental health care. We must strive to work on all these levels if we are to reduce the impact of mental ill-health, while nurturing the uniqueness and creativity of individuals."

Professor Patrick McGorry, AO MD PhD,
Executive Director
OYH Research Centre, University of Melbourne

Alfredo's Journey:

An Artist's Creative Life with Bipolar Disorder

by Alfredo Zotti

Modern History Press

Learn more at www.AlfredoZotti.com

Library of Congress Cataloging-in-Publication Data

Zotti, Alfredo, 1958- author.
  Alfredo's journey : an artist's creative life with bipolar disorder / by Alfredo Zotti.
      pages cm
  Includes bibliographical references and index.
  ISBN 978-1-61599-225-6 (hardcover : alk. paper) -- ISBN 978-1-61599-224-9 (pbk. : alk. paper) -- ISBN 978-1-61599-226-3 (ebook)
  1. Zotti, Alfredo, 1958---Mental health. 2. Manic-depressive persons--Psychology. 3. Manic-depressive illness--Treatment. 4. Counseling. I. Title.
  RC516.Z68 2014
  616.89'5--dc 3
                    2014002544

Modern History Press, an imprint of
Loving Healing Press
5145 Pontiac Trail
Ann Arbor, MI 48105

Tollfree USA/CAN: 888-761-6268
FAX 734-663-6861
info@ModernHistoryPress.com

Contents

Table of Poems ii

Table of Drawings and Sketches.. iii

Foreword v

PART I Alfredo's Journey... 1

Chapter 1 – Professionals, Sufferers, their Caregivers and the Public 3

Chapter 2 – The Therapist and the Client: A Matter of Trust.......... 9

Chapter 3 – Developing Critical Consciousness through Therapy... 17

Chapter 4 – The Therapy Intensifies…... 27

Chapter 5 – In Our Darkest Hour... We Start to See the Light 33

Chapter 6 – We'll meet again, don't know where........................... 47

PART II: Treatment and Critique 59

Chapter 7 – Spirituality and Coping with Mental Illness 61

Chapter 8 – Liberalism and its Human Nature.............................. 65

Chapter 9 – Clinical and Counseling Psychology 77

Chapter 10 – The Science and Art of Psychology.......................... 85

Chapter 11 – Cognitive Behavioral Therapy................................. 89

Chapter 12 – Childhood Traumatic Experiences 97

Chapter 13 – Internal and External Aspects of Multiple Personalities
in Bipolar Disorder 107

Chapter 14 – Antipsychotic and Antidepressant Drugs................. 111

Chapter 15 – Creativity and the Creative Artist........................... 121

    Discussion and Conclusion... 144

    What Creative Sufferers Have to Say...................................... 146

Chapter 16 – Heart Intelligence and the Creative Process............ 151

Chapter 17 – Disability—Don't Dismiss My Ability..................... 159

    Montmartre and Moulin Rouge 162

    Turn-of-the Century France and Lautrec's posters................... 164

Conclusion 167

References 173

References for Counseling and Clinical Psychology 175

References for Science and Art of Psychology 177

References for CBT and Social Anxiety 178

Article and Website 180

References for Antipsychotic and Antidepressants Drugs Essay 181

References 183

Index 185

Table of Poems

Digital Cities 13

Rozelle Hospital 40

Mindfulness 142

The Forgotten People 143

Table of Drawings and Sketches

Self-Portrait. iv

Alfredo (depicted at age 5) 10

Impression of Bob Rich, PhD. 22

Sally, the nurse 34

Rozelle Hospital's main entrance 43

The Venetian Tower at Rozelle Hospital................................. 44

Impression of Cheryl, my wife 53

"For the Love of Money" (Version A) 128

"For the Love of Money" (Version B)..................................... 129

The shell of an old tape cassette is now a business card holder......... 131

"The Face of Depression" (my father)................................... 133

Portrait of a dog 134

Portrait of Agnes.. 135

Morning Mist 142

Intrinsic Cardiac Ganglion seen through confocal microscope 152

Henri de Toulouse-Lautrec 160

Self-Portrait.
Drawing by Alfredo Zotti, 2006

Foreword

Alfredo Zotti is a highly unusual person. So, you are about to read a highly unusual book. It is full of wisdom and insight into the human condition in general, and into the joys, tribulations, and challenges of someone who experiences Bipolar Disorder.

To the world at large, Bipolar is a personal tragedy, a form of insanity that attracts stigma and irrational judgment. I was a counseling psychologist for 22 years, and learned that this is a matter of perspective. You can choose to focus in on the condition's negatives and suffer, or you can do as Alfredo has done, and construct a wonderful silver lining—even a rainbow lining—around the cloud. To Alfredo and me, Bipolar is neither good nor bad, but both. The ups and downs in mood are distressing, and they do impinge negatively on those around the person. However, they also lead to creativity, a different and illuminating view of the world, an opportunity to contribute to the welfare of others.

This is a matter of choice; only most people with Bipolar don't know they have that choice. If you have Bipolar, or someone important to you does, then you could change your life by following the story of Alfredo's. I don't mean that you should copy him, but rather to have him inspire you to stop looking at yourself as damaged.

An internet search will find many highly creative people who have contributed to the betterment of humankind, and who have been diagnosed with Bipolar. There are also historical figures who would have been diagnosed with Bipolar Disorder if they lived now. In cultures other than our own, this was true of many Shamans, seers, and spiritual leaders.

Alfredo is a humble man, who has turned what used to be his affliction into his tool for doing good. For many years now, he has posted on interactive websites, and answered thousands of emails from suffering people, entirely voluntarily. His "payment" has been the joy of giving, the highest form of benefit one can receive.

In this book, he tells his story: how he got to his current situation. As you follow him on his journey, you can enjoy his quirky humor, be stimulated by his insights, and inspired by his achievement. The advice

1 Professionals, Sufferers, their Caregivers and the Public

This book is written for mental health professionals, such as psychologists and psychiatrists, and also for people who suffer with a mental disorder. It is good for mental health professionals to understand the point of view of the client/patient. It is good for people with similar experiences to be able to identify with someone else who is in the same situation, and yet has built a good life with great satisfaction.

The book is about my experiences, or to be precise, my journey with Bipolar Disorder. Very seldom do sufferers write honestly about their experiences with mental disorders, mostly because of the stigma associated with disclosure. I have come to understand that if we don't come out of the closet and speak of our experiences, stigma will continue to affect our lives. The best way to fight stigma is adopting complete honesty and transparency so that people learn about us, our feelings, our abilities, and our hopes for the future.

I had a troubled childhood; I have experienced homelessness, have been in a psychiatric hospital—not because of suffering with some serious mental disorder, but because of being homeless—and became a friend to many people with psychoses, such as schizophrenia. I later started to study psychology at a university so that I could better help people with mental disorders online.

Now I have created an online monthly journal. The *Anti Stigma Crusaders Journal* (ASC) attempts to give an inside view into mental disorders from the perspective of those who suffer from them. Bipolar Disorder can be either a positive force in society or a negative one. It is up to all of us to help sufferers with Bipolar Disorder and other mental disorders as well, so that they may feel included and motivated to contribute to their society.

Many famous people are known to have behaved in ways consistent with a diagnosis of Bipolar Disorder. It would be difficult to include the many names here, but Winston Churchill, Abraham Lincoln, Beethoven, Michelangelo, van Gogh, and many other geniuses appear to have had symptoms and moods consistent with Bipolar Disorder. Research has shown a clear link between genius and madness. I here include a quote, which is from an advertisement made for Apple Computers, written by Rob Siltanen and Ken Segall and narrated by Richard Dreyfuss, who suffers with Bipolar Disorder. I really like the words. If only politicians and affluent people understood the message of the advertisement, the world would be a much better place. It goes like this:

> Here's to the crazy ones. The misfits. The rebels. The trouble-makers. The round pegs in the square holes. The ones who see things differently. They're not fond of rules. And they have no respect for the status quo. You can quote them, disagree with them, glorify or vilify them. About the only thing you can't do is ignore them. Because they change things. They push the human race forward. And while some may see them as the crazy ones, we see genius. Because the people who are crazy enough to think they can change the world are the ones who do.

This book is divided into two sections: in the first part (my personal story), I write about my past experiences, particularly as an inpatient of Rozelle Hospital in a suburb of Sydney, Australia, and my struggle with mental illness; in the second part (current knowledge of the disorder), I look at my voluntary work in my attempt to help people and myself. What is this thing that we call mental illness? This is what I attempt to answer in the second part of this book.

This is my story and I emphasize "story," because all humans are storied beings. This means that we make sense of our lives by telling ourselves a story about ourselves. The best that humanity has to offer, in terms of emotions, feelings, hopes, and struggles can be found by reading stories of those who have left us books like *To Kill a Mockingbird* (Harper Lee), *A Room of One's Own* (Virginia Woolf), and *Pedagogy of the Oppressed* (Paolo Freire). Literature, especially novels and personal stories, can tell us a lot about what it is like to be human. Indeed, I believe that there is a strong connection between good novelists and psychologists and in the future, I would like to see better communication and co-operation between these two professions.

While all of the information presented here is real and accurate, I have introduced in the story the fictional character of "Stella," who in part represents my mother, whom I lost to bowel cancer when I was 18. She was just 40 years of age and died a few months after surgery, in the early 1980s. She also represents my spirit—that part of me that has become self-critical and that tries very hard to control the child in me, the child that has been so hurt in the past that complete development has not been possible until recently. Stella also represents the best therapists that I have met in my life. Altogether, she is a complex ensemble of help—both self-help and the help of mental health professionals and other good people I have found on my journey.

Stella features in many parts of this first section, and while some readers may find her presence strange or out of place, given that this character is part of my imagination, it is nevertheless important in that it helps me personify that part of my spirit that watches over me and guides me as in the mind watching over itself. I still have a long way to go to fully recover. Indeed, many people do not fully develop and remain slaves of their child selves, which very often causes problems because of runaway emotions, uncontrolled moods, and related problems.

In the story, Stella is my imaginary therapist, a beautiful and intelligent middle-aged woman, who is very compassionate and who, in my mind, can make up for that void inside of me that was created when my parents, especially my mother, abandoned me. They travelled throughout Europe, to work, leaving me behind with various relatives, sometimes for years.

It is true to say that while we all have many different aspects to our personalities, we also have a parent, a child, and a self personality. These aspects of personality are sometimes well-integrated to make a person really whole and these people often find happiness and stability in life. But for many of us, who suffer with a mental disorder, these three aspects of personality are not well integrated and are sometimes detached from each other. In Dr. Thomas Harris' book *I'm OK, You're OK: A Practical Guide to Transactional Analysis* (1969), he wrote extensively about the child-parent-self aspects of personalities. I think that this book is still very relevant to those who suffer with Bipolar Disorder or depression and probably all mental disorders.

What I can say, after writing this book, which is an account of my journey as someone who suffers with *Bipolar II Disorder*[1], is that I am learning to cope with the disorder. Indeed, my portrait is not on page *vi* because of vanity, but because it indicated an attempt to look at my spirit closely, just like someone looks at one's face in the mirror. Not only am I learning to cope with Bipolar Disorder, but I also use it to fuel my creativity and to help others.

---

[1] *Bipolar II Disorder* is characterized by at least one episode of hypomania and at least one episode of major depression. Diagnosis for Bipolar II disorder requires that the individual must never have experienced a full manic episode (one manic episode meets the criteria for Bipolar I disorder). Berk, M. & Dodd, S. (2005)

I help other sufferers by writing on many websites. However, I am not always received well by the members of self-help websites who suffer with mental disorders, such as Bipolar Disorder, Major Depression, Dysthymia, Dissociative Identity Disorder (DID), or Schizophrenia, to name a few. I think that I have the tendency to expose very difficult and sensitive issues that many sufferers like to avoid. I know that the only way to develop, to integrate our child personality with the rest of us, and to become able to control our disorder is by being completely transparent with ourselves, to have courage and to have the ability to be self-critical, the kind of self-criticism that Paolo Freire, the famous Brazilian educator, called "Critical Consciousness." I don't necessarily help people on websites by agreeing with them and by trying to make them feel better. Of course, I try to do this whenever possible; but my real intention is to awaken the critical consciousness so that a sufferer can start to liberate their soul and possibly begin to find their way in the Universe. Some become annoyed and distance themselves from me. That is fine; but others continue the dialogue with me, and together we often make good progress in terms of under-standing our mental disorder.

What I am trying to answer in this book is this: What is Bipolar Disorder? I can only answer (and I will answer it at the end of the book) by relying on my personal experience, knowing that it may not apply to everyone's story: I was just a very sensitive and creative child. This is not a genetic defect but a genetic gift. Because of being sensitive, when my parents abandoned me, Bipolar was triggered. For me, it is not a genetic problem, unless being talented and sensitive is a problem. In my case, it is an emotional problem, a kind of anguish that never goes away. This anguish causes symptoms that very often accompany us throughout life.

People like me may need medication to deal with the emotional prob-lems, symptoms, and moods; but the fact remains that we have no proof that mental disorders, even the most serious ones, are purely genetic or biological. There will always be genetic, biological, and environmental factors at work and, for this reason, we need to treat mental disorders by using a bio-psychosocial approach—that is, to attend to biological, social, and psychological problems.

I fear that this is not always the case today, where many people opt for medication first, forgetting how difficult it is to control Bipolar and what it really takes to get better. In my opinion, the mind can be a powerful tool in the control and maintenance of our disorder, but the problem is that because of ideology and various other social problems, many of us are unable to help ourselves and tend to give up.

Genes can be switched on and off in the environment, but emotions and fears need to be understood, controlled, helped, and released when the time is right. For this, there is a need for extensive therapy and the "will" of the sufferer to participate in the therapy, to be willing to face up to memories and facts that may be painful. The aim should always be to develop resilience.

For example, mania in Bipolar Disorder is a kind of overconfidence in the face of disaster. As Michael Corry and Ann Tubridy once wrote in their book, *Going MAD? Understanding Mental Illness* (2001), it's like rearranging the deck chairs of the sinking Titanic and even inviting people to continue the party while the ship is about to go down into the deep ocean. It is partly fear of failure. Depression can be the opposite, or fear of living and the desire to give up. Medication can help a person sometimes, although very rarely, even for life; but it is like using crutches to walk while others can learn to walk without them. Some can learn to cope without medication.

To get to the bottom of the problems, however, we have to deal with emotions, and this requires that both the sufferer and the therapist enter into a very deep and honest dialogue with the intention of changing the personality to a more resilient one. That is why I am a fan of humanistic psychology and an admirer of the late Carl Rogers' theories. Unfortunately, one-size-fits-all methods will not do, so good psychologists have to rely on the best that theories and methods have to offer. I am proud that I have been able to confront my problems and my past in the attempt to rationalize the problems so that I can become in control, rather than be controlled by runaway emotions based on non-factual fears. Some irrational thoughts will always be there, but I am aware of them and I can do something about them. That is the development of critical consciousness, or the mind watching over the mind.

I write my story much as a writer would write about other people. In this sense, I try to look at myself from a distance. To what extent I've succeeded, I cannot say.

2 | The Therapist and the Client: A Matter of Trust

Stella Ferguson is an attractive, motherly, middle-aged woman. She is a therapist and also a multi-talented person. She was playing piano at the age of six and is also a visual artist. She writes poems and has published a number of self-help books. Her clients are mainly wealthy people but she does bulk bill (meaning that she charges the government at a lower hourly rate to treat poor people).

I remember the first day when I went to therapy. Stella was sitting on her comfortable black leather armchair, resting her chin on her fist while taking a break from her busy day, probably in an attempt to give her busy mind a break. Nat King Cole was quietly singing in the background, "There will never be another you," and the blinds were semi-closed, letting little sunlight through the windows. I was to become one of her clients, but also a good friend.

There was no infatuation or romance between Stella and me. We respected each other, almost forgetting that we were the opposite sex, and built a strong and transparent friendship, something that I feel is necessary for successful therapy to happen. In fact, the most powerful thing in therapy is friendship. In my opinion, ditch the Watsonian and Skinnerian ideology about behavioral modification, more suited to animal training than people. Instead, embrace the ideas of Carl Rogers and his unconditional respect for the client, and let the client find their own way, without pressure, in an atmosphere of friendship. Our mutual respect was due to the fact that we are both gifted in many ways. Both Stella and I are married to other people and our relationship was a rare friendship that was taking us on a journey of self-discovery and self-awareness.

The initial therapy sessions were quite formal and it took me quite a while to open up. I could discuss other people's problems quite easily, but not mine. Stella seemed quite frustrated about it because, as she told me, I desperately needed to let my emotions out and this could only happen if I found the courage to confront my traumatic past. As the sessions and the months went by, I found myself able to open up and begin to tell my life story, something that I found very therapeutic.

While Stella was thinking, she suddenly felt emotional, reaching for the tissue box on the little table near her (usually it is the client that cries and reaches for the tissue box). She told me that what had brought up the emotions was her recollection of the sixth session she'd had with me, a session that I will never forget. Stella recalled the drawing that I had shown her in one of our sessions, which I had made when I was about six years of age. It was the drawing of a lonely child, sitting on a huge chair in the middle of a large, empty room. This symbolized the tremendous void inside me that had built up because I had been abandoned—a void that, as I told her, would never be filled.

Alfredo (depicted at age 5)

I had told Stella about my interest in childhood traumas. Because of my volunteer work online, in my attempt to help people in all corners of the world, and with the help of counseling psychologist, Dr. Bob Rich, I had come to understand that what we call mental illness is mostly triggered by traumatic experiences. I believe that about 80 to 85% of all mental illness in the world is due to trauma, especially childhood trauma; and the people I helped online were and still are confirming this. Hundreds of people had experienced some sort of trauma, mostly during childhood, and sometimes in adulthood. Sometimes sufferers were aware of the trauma; but at other times, they were not. The interesting thing is that the traumatic experience would surface sooner or later. I had shown Stella many emails of sufferers who were telling me the stories about their childhood traumas. Here is what a young woman told me and we later found out that she had, indeed, experienced childhood trauma:

> I don't think there is a cause for my depression and psy-chosis. I was sexually assaulted at 16 and my mother was an alcoholic who suffered with Bipolar Disorder, and she was abusive and violent. But there does not seem to be any ongoing trauma from that.

I consulted my friend Dr. Bob Rich, who is a counseling psychologist, and he wrote:

> That kind of pattern makes me strongly suspect repressed severe trauma. She should go to a good therapist and do age regression hypnosis. If there is trauma, and she recalls it, she can deal with it and get rid of the problem sometimes for life. It usually feels too scary to do. I say to my clients: there is a box there, and you are working hard to keep the lid on. But what's in the box is not a monster. It's the photograph or movie of the monster. A photograph or movie cannot hurt you; only remind you of the past hurt.

Stella was very interested in my research and I could see that she enjoyed discussing my emails and the fact that I attempted to help so many people from all corners of the world. If nothing else, my care and company were therapeutic to many sufferers with mental disorders. It was that special friendship that we had built over time that really helped both me and the person I was trying to help or comfort, simply by listening without judgment and only giving advice if I had experience of the problem from a non-authoritarian position, the position of an equal sufferer. This worked very well. Of course, it did cause confrontations at times and sometimes the friendship was affected to the point that it had to be discontinued. But I feel that confrontation is good, just as much as support and agreement, because it stimulates the person to think and to change, even if this happens at a later date.

Change does not happen without some struggle, and verbal confrontation is a way in which people can unload their bottled-up emotions and feelings. Many unpleasant things have happened to me and at times, I have had to abandon some websites for disturbing their "peace" with my thought-provoking ideas. Sometimes I was banned from sites for demanding transparency and freedom of speech; but most of the times, I have been welcomed and achieved good things. I feel that this was all valuable effort because people tend to reflect on things even after such a confrontation. Such confrontation often brings to the surface childhood traumatic experiences.

Stella told me that she was in agreement with Dr. Bob Rich and now that she got to read the research that I had completed, she was really beginning to think of the possibility that childhood trauma could possibly make up most of what we call mental illness. After all, the majority of her clients (about 85%) had experienced childhood trauma, as she told me.

It was unreal for me to find that all of the sufferers with whom I was in contact would sooner or later identify their trauma simply by communicating with me openly. Perhaps my art served to break the ice. Or maybe it was my very open nature. My friendliness and openness emerged because of my own trauma. I had such a void inside, caused by the separation anxiety that I needed to communicate with people at a deeper level as much as possible. Communication was helping me and it was also helping others. The sharing of my art was a special thing for me. I loved to share my poems, my visual art and my music with people.

Even Stella found the poem that I had written and given to her, expressing how I felt while attempting to help others online—interesting and touching. I loved to share my creativity with Stella, who well understood me because she was aware that I expressed myself not only with words but also with poems, visual art, and music. Stella loved my art and she encouraged me to share it with her, to show her all that I did. This was part of the therapy. Here is the poem that I gave Stella to read:

Digital Cities

Journey through the digital cities of broken dreams,
wandering along the sites of sorrow
trying to touch the quantum hearts
that travel through the phone-lines.
The journey is long, the dream worth it.
To all the broken hearts who hide behind their anguish
my message is one of hope and love.
Hide no more and show your heart
for only then will your broken dreams turn into hope.

It was my visits to various websites that helped me realize that I needed help and that I could possibly find this help simply by communicating with other sufferers. We had a special understanding and insight into our disorders that many experts did not have or understand. Over the years, I have collected many emails from sufferers, which I have filed on computer and which I often read. Here are some of the emails:

> Alfredo, you asked why I thought people aren't forthcoming about sharing childhood experiences of abuse. I was thinking about that and realized that I didn't even think I had been abused until I was about 40. I always thought the depression was biochemical or the fault of someone or something else. Even then, there was a lot of shame just because of the thought of speaking ill of one's parents, or "blaming" them. I could always hear my mother's voice in my head whenever I thought or felt anything negative about her or my dad. Therapy has helped a lot with that and only in looking back can I see what I didn't know then.

My research, a questionnaire to over 100 therapists (out of nearly 2000 I had contacted worldwide), resulted in an estimate that childhood trauma makes up an average of 75% of all mental disorders. The therapists unanimously agreed that childhood trauma makes up a great percentage of all mental illness. In other words, stop the trauma and many would not develop a mental illness. Perhaps, without childhood trauma, mental illness as we know it would be a thing of the past. And while some people develop a mental illness due to mild trauma, sufferers usually have a history of severe and repeated trauma like physical abuse, sexual abuse, or other serious experiences. Indeed, I was fortunate to have helped people with severe Post Traumatic Stress Disorder (PTSD). I even wrote a song about a friend who later recovered but still suffers with some symptoms of schizophrenia. Here are the lyrics of the song which I wrote and gave Stella to read:

> Daisy was only 17 when she came to me.
> She had swollen lips and a bloodied shirt.
> Daisy tried to speak to me but her voice just failed.
> She'd been raped by her old man,
> he'd been riding her for some time.
> Daisy came to me with swollen eyes,
> she had been crying all day long, and she said:
> "What do I do now? What do I say?
> I can't go on this way, I can't go on."
> And I said: "Daisy, you must pick up the pieces,
> you must go on now, I'll help you all I can
> I'll stand by you."
> So we went to the police to tell her story, and I could see,
> Daisy would never be the same again.

In one session, Stella asked, "Is our world toxic to our children? Are we making our children sick? Are we creating mental illness in the process?" These are the kinds of questions that your research is bringing up in my mind, Alfredo." She read another email that my friend Judy had sent me and reading this increased her concerns:

> Alfredo, I really do agree with you here and I have asked myself this same question many times—What do we do? It is so frustrating to see this cycle of child abuse go on, generation after generation. I think those of us who are dealing with our depression or whatever have been able to see where it comes from and to try to heal ourselves and, hopefully, make sure we don't keep passing this on. Those who hurt us were also hurt as children, I believe.
>
> But there is still that stigma among many about mental illness, so nobody wants to talk about it or about their abusive childhoods; so people still remain ignorant about what effect it has. I think most criminals have also most likely suffered some kind of abuse or mistreatment in their lives. I guess I would rather be depressed than be a murderer, but think of all the suffering we could avoid if we could stop the mistreatment of children. A lot of people don't even recognize abuse when they see it; we've gotten so immune to it. They don't realize that words *can* hurt us, a lot of times worse than any physical punishment. I know that as a child, I sometimes would wish my dad

would just hit me and get it over with, rather than rant on and on about how stupid and disgusting I was; we all were.

What do we do? Right now, I'd say we do what we are doing—trying to heal ourselves so that we can keep our children from having to suffer because of our pain. Somehow, I wish we could bring this subject out into the light where everyone could see it and people could be educated so that if they suspect it is happening to a child they know, they may step in. It's so widespread, it's easy to feel despair; but it's just like so many other things—we can just do it one step at a time. I think you've brought up a very important topic—I know it's not the first time you've talked about it, but you asked *the question: what do we do???* We need more answers.

Stella was coming to understand, while helping me, that childhood trauma is much neglected and that society needs to pay more attention to it if we are serious about reducing mental illness. Prevention is better than cure. Let's reduce childhood trauma and put most of our world resources in doing this, rather than focusing exclusively on spending money on drug research and various other things that seem to fuel mental illness rather than check it. In many ways, I feel that we are creating mental illness in our world.

"My God," Stella said, "if childhood trauma is what causes most mental illness, then we are covering this up subconsciously, blaming the whole thing on biological defects and genetics. That is what we are doing. We are basically saying that mental illness is a biological/ genetic problem even though we know that it is much more complex than that and that many call for a bio-psycho-social approach. But our actions don't seem to support the bio-psycho-social model."

Stella was aware that I was not in agreement with Scientology, which is totally against any kind of medication. No, not at all, because I know that medication can save lives. After all, my wife suffers with *Bipolar I*[2] and she does need medication, every day. At the same time, the practice of medicating people when they do not need it is still a problem. Medication can also be harmful and the world needs to be more cautious about the greed of pharmaceutical corporations and their influences in universities

---

[2] *Bipolar I* disorder sometimes occurs along with episodes of hypomania or major depression as well. It is a type of Bipolar Disorder, and conforms to the classic concept of manic-depressive illness, which can include psychosis during mood episodes. The difference with Bipolar II disorder is that the latter requires that the individual must never have experienced a full manic episode—only less severe hypomanic episode(s). Berk, M. & Dodd, S. (2005).

and government organizations. Much research is ringing alarm bells. There is evidence to suggest that childhood abuse affects a great number of our children. A survey from my personal longitudinal research of nine years has revealed that about 75% of sufferers, out of a sample of over 700, have endured traumatic experiences during their childhood. For example, many people who suffer with Borderline Personality Disorder (BPD) report having had a history of abuse and neglect. Many studies support these claims, as we will see in the second part of this book, and that childhood trauma is a risk factor for a diagnosis of Schizophrenia, Major Depression, Personality Disorders, and Bipolar Disorder later in life. Some research indicates that childhood trauma is a causal factor for the development of psychosis and schizophrenia.

Taking medication does not mean that mental disorders are necessarily a purely biological dysfunction. We don't know yet. This is the chicken and egg question: is there an initial genetic defect, a predisposition, where a traumatic environmental event triggers a mental illness? Or is it the trauma that changes biological functions? And what about, as I often suggest, the possibility that some people are much more sensitive and creative than others (meaning that this cannot be seen as a genetic defect) and, therefore, develop a mental disorder because of their sensitivities? Indeed, many of these sensitive people often gravitate to the creative professions so that they can do therapy through their work. These are the helping professions. After many discussions, I sensed that my concerns for people with mental disorders and childhood trauma had struck a major chord with Stella. There was such overwhelming evidence that childhood trauma causes mental illness! And with the statistics giving such alarming figures, it was not difficult to speculate by an informed and educated position that childhood trauma made up most of what we call mental illness today.

3 Developing Critical Consciousness through Therapy

Alfredo: "I am sorry Stella, I'm a little late."

Stella: "Come in Alfredo. Sit down, please. What's been happening lately?"

[That is the question I was to hear every time I went to therapy. Yet I knew that what had been happening lately was always a roller coaster of moods, symptoms and inner pain, something that I have learned to live with. It never goes away and it has become part of my personality; those of us with severe mental disorders simply learn to live with it, but I think that the idea of a plastic brain is also overrated. The brain is plastic, but it is not always possible to change behavior and thoughts that have been established over many years. It is not as simple as that.]

Alfredo: "Well, I have been thinking about my past, Stella. My life has been full of traumatic experiences and my mind is fragile now, even though, as the years go on, I become wiser and more resilient. But I feel that my mind is very delicate. I must be careful. I've got to take it easy with everything I do and my focus is on striking a balance."

Stella: "Anything in particular that you've been concerned with?"

Alfredo: "Yes, I was thinking about the time when I started to self-harm by burning my arm with a lit cigarette, causing huge blisters. I am concerned because I am in touch with many people who inflict self-harm and I know all about that. I still have the scars today. Here, look."

[I pulled up my shirt sleeves, showing the scars to Stella.]

Stella: "Oh my, these scars are not very visible now, unless one looks closely; but I can imagine that years ago they must have been noticeable. Why did you do that?"

Alfredo: "Not something I can explain in a couple of words. I would like to tell you a few things before I get to my self-harming and I do need to tell you this to get things off my chest. I will go back in time a little to give you a better idea. It was the early 80s and life was good to me. I was finally living with my family. I had been living with them since we came to Australia. As soon as we arrived, back in the early 70s, we were sent to work in a wood factory. We were working there for a year or two and then my father gradually started to play music in various night clubs, on weekends. He was an orchestra conductor in Europe, quite famous, but he had gambled all of his fortune away and he was also an alcoholic. He had lost the respect of his colleagues and no one would give him work because he was almost always drunk. Fortunately, when we came here, he stopped drinking excessively, although there were always periods of severe intoxication. He suffered with depression and the creative anguish that affects all great artists. He was self-medicating with alcohol and this is often what substance abuse is all about, a way to self-medicate. It often ends up making things worse, though, because alcohol, though helpful while you are under its effects, later becomes a depressant.

My father and I never got along. We had a kind of hate/hate relationship were he took all of his frustration out on me, my brother, and my mother. He probably did love us in his own way, but alcohol transformed him into a problematic child. He was not violent, though he could break furniture and put up tantrums when he wanted to, keeping us all up at night. But he could hurt us psychologically and words can be just as painful as physical violence."

As I was telling this to Stella, I suddenly felt a great pain inside. I hadn't realized until then how painful these memories could be. It really hurt, just as if I was revisiting those traumatic days. Anxiety was rising and now my heart was pumping unusually fast. And I can see how painful it must be for sufferers to go over their traumatic past and how difficult to tell their miserable story to a therapist, often a stranger. Lucky that Stella was not a stranger; she was a friend, and I feel that there is need for some sort of friendship or deeper relationship with the therapist if positive change is to take place. In this sense, I really love humanistic psychology and the work of Carl Rogers and Maslow, and their work is important and meaningful to us sufferers.

[There was silence for a few seconds and I thought to myself: therapy exists between art and science, not in science alone, and I feel that Rogers, Maslow, and even Freud add elements of the artistic side of therapy that Cognitive Behavioral Therapy (CBT) or other scientifically based methods cannot.]

Stella: "Was there something in particular that your father disliked about you?"

Alfredo: "Yes, he did not want me to become a musician or a visual artist. He believed that that kind of life was not good and because he had had such a hard time with it, he thought that I would experience problems, as well. He prevented me from playing the piano by locking his room to keep me from getting to the grand piano and took away all of my art materials. That was really hurtful and traumatic for me because I could no longer express my pain now and I felt totally unwell. Not being allowed to play the piano, draw, or paint with oils or watercolor was the same as stopping my breath itself. I needed music and visual art to survive. These creative expressions are part of me, Stella, and I cannot separate them from my personality, especially because I have synesthesia. I express myself not only with words, but also with music and visual art, and this gets me into trouble sometimes. Art is a language for me, a language that can express deep emotions and feelings and one that many people do not speak or understand these days."

Stella: "Yes, I can understand that, Alfredo. I am a multi-talented artist like you, as you know, and it is hard for people to understand that creativity is an important part of our life. So what happened next? I mean, how did you get to play the piano if your father had locked the piano room?"

Alfredo: "I remember when my father locked the room. It was so painful. The only thing that was good about my life—music—was now being taken away from me. How could a father be so cruel and insensitive? Strange emotions had developed inside, so strange that crying and feeling anxious had become a relief valve for me and very much part of my problematic personality. I could see that I was on the road to becoming just like my father.

It was my mother who opened the room when my father went out or went away for a few days. Thank God that my mother had the intelligence to give me access to the piano. Because of that, I later became a well-respected jazz and classical pianist. I think that music became a great love and therapy for me, and made my life so meaningful that I started to think that all the suffering was worth it.

I became a musician, a piano player working at Hunters Lodge in Double Bay. It was a well-known restaurant and I played six nights per week with a trio: upright grand piano, double bass, and drums. We were all young and good-looking. We had a lovely little jazz trio and many good musicians occasionally came to see us play. It was an important place in those days, people like Al Martino and other famous entertainers came to dine and listen to the music there. We played till the late hours of the night, sometimes 1 or 2 AM. I was very happy and I loved the job.

At that time, I had met a nice lady who later became my fiancé; she was a very good jazz singer. Life was good for a while, until my mother developed bowel cancer and died. My father had to sell our house to pay for the trip back to Italy where my mother had wanted to be buried. So he went back to Italy with my younger brother. My family left for Italy but I stayed behind. That was a good excuse to get away from my father. Our relationship was toxic.

My father eventually came back to Sydney, remarried a lovely Italian / Egyptian lady, Paola, who is today my stepmother, and we found the way to put the past behind us so that before he died from liver failure, I forgave him and we had a good discussion in the hospital where he was residing. That was interesting because, after ten years of not seeing my father, I decided to ring him up because I had a feeling that something was wrong. My hunch was right; he was dying. But that is another story. At least he had changed a little and for a few years, he drank much less, but the damage to his body had been done. Alcohol and nicotine can be a terrible combination in the long term."

Stella: "Let's explore your concept of forgiveness and its effect on you. Did forgiving your father improve anything about your life? Did that change your perspective on life?"

[I burst into tears. I again felt a lot of pain being released from my body. I could almost see the imagined dark vapor coming out of my chest. That was like a poison, a poison that had eaten away at me for so long. My inability to forgive had contributed greatly to my mental disorder and when I was finally able to forgive, it took away so much pain. Yet there was a lot of pain still left, though it was a little different.]

Alfredo: "Definitely, Stella. By forgiving my father, I opened the door to a new life, a new way of understanding the world. My father was an artist in pain. He did the best he could under very difficult circumstances and he was also sensitive and gifted in many ways. But, just like he mistreated me, his father had treated him terribly and so, in turn, he did the same to me; he treated me terribly. Fathers treat their children as they have been treated by their own father, with some exceptions, of course. It is a vicious circle that sometimes never ends and keeps on going from generation to generation."

Stella: "Why did you become homeless, Alfredo? Someone talented like you should not be homeless! And what sort of thoughts were you having at that time?"

Alfredo: "I had simply given up, just as in the concept of 'freeze, fight, and flight,' I had become frozen, unable to do anything or go on anymore. Too much trauma! I needed others to take care of me or alternatively, die out as in the idea of survival of the fittest.

I had some savings from working at Hunters Lodge, but the money soon ended and I lost the job because of being depressed and unable to play music anymore. We all lost the job and the band split up because there was no way that we could replace even one member of the band. We had become a unit, three members that made a whole. It was a very good jazz trio. At the time, we used to play George Benson, Boz Scaggs, Billy Joel, and Elton John—many of the now-classic pieces like *Candle in the Wind*. That was the top of my music career because I was a respected pianist who could play as well as the best-American piano players. And the funny thing is that I was a self-taught musician.

I had developed a great knowledge of harmonies. I knew all the chord combinations and this was something that many musicians envied in me. I had perfect pitch and could hear music in my mind. I could write for an orchestra without needing an instrument. I never had a teacher and my father did his best to prevent me from playing. But I knew the piano well and I was a born musician. I probably was a piano player in a past life. I know that this will sound strange to those who don't believe in past lives, but how else would I have such knowledge of the piano without a single lesson in my life? I also became a good music arranger and I could write music for full orchestras. This is not the kind of knowledge that one learns on his/her own, because knowledge of each orchestra instrument is required. So it remains a mystery to me. Today I compose music with my computer and I know what all of the instruments of an orchestra can do. I play all instruments though my piano keyboard attached to a computer and I can imitate a full orchestra with amazing results because it is pretty hard to distinguish real instruments from the ones I imitate, thanks to the technology and my skills. I was able to get the eighth grade of pianoforte Diploma at the conservatorium without having had a single lesson and without a single music teacher in my life. I could play the complex classical pieces that only accomplished musicians can."

Stella: "What else was concerning you around that time Alfredo?"

Alfredo: "My fiancé and I separated because she did not understand depression and could not cope with it, and I certainly was unwell. My moods could be terrible at times; the (hypo)mania, especially, could cause problems in that I would often become antisocial, or just upset people with my unusual and overbearing behavior. I was mostly a negative person. However, I was never violent and never hurt anyone physically in my life. If I hurt someone psychologically, it is because I was hurt psychologically and because that is what traumatized people often do, which is to lash out at others and for me, given that I had never been violent, lashing out at people verbally was a way to get some frustration out.

Trauma after trauma, my mental disorder was becoming worse. There was no doubt that I was suffering with Post Traumatic Stress Disorder and

Impression of Bob Rich, PhD.
Drawing by Alfredo Zotti

that it was my main problem, which manifested with symptoms of Bipolar Disorder. But for that trauma to be released, I had to wait for Bob Rich because when he came into my life, back in 2007, that was when I started to let all of the emotions out. Bob is a very experienced psychologist and he understood that I had a very good heart and that I was a talented and sensitive man. He wanted to help me and he dedicated four years of his life, while doing other things, of course, to help me. The man has donated hours of his life to help me though I was a perfect stranger to him. The funny thing is that we have never met in person but have become email friends. I never dreamed that one could find such a wonderful friendship in cyberspace. I think that Bob and I share something special: we care for the world and the people, and this is the real gift, I feel; this is what it means to be gifted, to care about and help our world. Bob does not like to be called gifted, but how else you define someone like Bob? Only a gifted man can help others to heal. I rather think of Bob as a modern Shaman rather than a psychologist. The idea of a Shaman is more appealing to me."

Stella: "What kind of problems did your mania cause you, Alfredo?"

Alfredo: "I could do some pretty terrible things, like shoplifting, drunk driving, smoking pot, and lying to people."

Stella: "Did you ever get caught for stealing or shoplifting?"

Alfredo: "Almost always; but for some reason, the judges knew that I was not well and that I was a good person who was suffering with some kind of mental disorder. Who in their right mind steals a pen from a supermarket while video cameras are on? Yes, I knew there were video cameras there, but I did it anyway. I needed the adrenaline rush and I wanted to do something wrong toward self-sabotage, in order to upset myself, those around me, and the system. That was hate, hate for the world. I was not violent, so that is how I could retaliate. At that moment, I was suffering with Agitated Depression, which is different from the Vegetative depression."

Stella: "What do you mean by Agitated Depression? Is it different from the Vegetative Depression? How?"

Alfredo: "My agitated depression is different in that I become anxious, still quite energetic, but very much in inner turmoil. I need to do things but I develop a great resentment inside toward greedy people, our troubled social world, and those politicians and powerful people who make life such a misery for so many others. Greed is the root of all evil. When I feel like that, reality can be distorted and situations can be misinterpreted. I guess that this is the kind of inner torment experienced before the "break"—that the situation is similar to that which triggered the mental disorder in the first place. It remains with us and it is a kind of panic state mixed with depression. Giving antidepressants to people with agitated depression, in my opinion, is not going to help them at all. It would probably add to the state of agitation. But I also suffer with vegetative depression. Today, with the help of Bob Rich, I have come to understand that I can control both types of depression, although this is not an easy thing to do. I cannot take any antidepressants because they trigger mania in me. I just take a minimum dose of anticonvulsants (Epilim) to avoid (hypo)mania."

Stella: "Can you give me an example of how you help yourself, Alfredo?"

Alfredo: "Yes, sure! When the vegetative depression strikes, it basically tells me to give up on life and stay in bed. And I really do believe this silent, inner voice of the depression. I do feel the need to give up, to ruminate. I have absolutely no energy to do anything. Even the slightest movement is an effort. There is great anxiety inside and I feel as if the end of the world is nearing. But I know that this is an illusion of my mind arising from my past traumas. So I need to do the opposite of what this inner voice tells me to do. If it tells me to give up and stay in bed, I do the opposite; I get up and try to do normal things I usually do when I am reasonably well. At first, it's like walking with a chain on my legs or being restrained in some way. Movement is difficult and painful and the initial attempts are the hardest. I used to fail at this in the beginning. But now I have been able to conquer this depression and can function reasonably well. It takes a lot of knowledge, self awareness, determination, and strength. It is not just CBT, but much more than that. It is the mind watching over itself."

Stella: "How well can you control your vegetative depression?"

Alfredo: "Well, I can function within my limits. I cannot take on too much. Upsets or disappointments can be triggers for major mood swings, so that I need to be careful. I can only function well in a supportive environment. In contemporary Australia, universities are much more aware of mental disorders and things have changed. Many academics have a greater understanding today, and I know this because I studied at university about fifteen years ago, when I got my degree in social anthropology, at the same University of Newcastle. Back then, it was nothing like today; there was a lot of prejudice. Today, we simply have too many students with mental disorders and things are changing by necessity."

Stella: "We have come to the end of the session Alfredo. We'll continue next week and I hope that you will tell me more about your experience with the university."

[As I left Stella's practice, I was thinking about my time in college. For me, it had been a real struggle because it was the studies that helped me to look at myself critically and to give me the courage to revisit my traumatic past. I was studying sociology and later psychology and it was logical that sooner or later I would turn a critical eye on myself to find what I am trying to explain in this book. I believe that it was my spirit that had been broken, not just the brain that had been affected. The brain's wiring and chemistry can be affected by a broken spirit when someone loses the will to live, to go on and to fight for another day. Life is a constant fight, a struggle, no matter how we sugar-coat things.]

4 The Therapy Intensifies...

I was walking to Stella's clinic, having finally found parking for my car, and I was thinking about my days at the university as a student. I was preparing myself to discuss this with Stella. I went back, in my mind, to a time when I enrolled for my Master's degree and went to the department bright and early for the introductory session for new graduate students. There I had strange thoughts running through my mind. I thought to myself: "These people have such a middleclass view of the world and their ideas are so far removed from my world." I was struggling to find a common ground and I wondered if this was also a cultural problem, given that I am an Italian immigrant.

To me, it felt as if these people were all on the same wavelength of thought, following an academic ideology that did not seem to work in the world which I had experienced. They had an answer for everything, even issues that defy explanation. I felt that this was unkind for me to think this way, that maybe I was looking from a problematic perspective. We are all different, after all, and we need different people with different views to make the world go 'round. But I still felt that many academics did not have a well-developed heart and by this I mean that they lacked empathy, compassion, and wisdom—things that are more in tune with the human spirit than academic intellectualism.

Of course, I understand now that not all academic are the same though I would be tempted to say that the majority do lack empathy. The reality is that professors need to operate within the system, a system that is very restrictive in terms of spiritual understanding or anything that is not based on empirical evidence. I must say that having become friends with some academics, especially professors and older academics, I can say that many are on my wavelength it is just that they cannot function on this wavelength in an increasingly controlled and strict university environment. This is strange given that the very idea of a university embodies an institution capable of challenging even the most empirical and established knowledge. Unfortunately, even universities have their own fixed ideology.

I was finally in the waiting room but decided to take my mind off the university for a while and pick up a book. Of course, as soon as I did that, Stella called me in.

Stella: "Please sit down, Alfredo, and tell me what has been happening lately."

Alfredo: "I will pick up the discussion from where we left off about the university. I think that I became unwell when I started my Master's degree. The studies were too much for me and a major depression was triggered. There was some stigma at the time and I was a bit of a fool for disclosing my Bipolar II disorder so openly, back in those days. But fortunately, today things have improved a little. Stigma can still be found but I guess that I am also stronger now and I don't let it get to me. I have been able to externalize the stigma so that I don't see it from an inner perspective, something which can be dangerous because it often leads to suicide."

Stella: "What do you mean?"

Alfredo: "Well, we can see stigma everywhere if we are not able to externalize it. In the old days, when people treated me with disdain, I felt that this was because I was faulty and deserved it and, of course, this led to depression. Now, if they do so, I know it's because they have faulty attitudes and it's nothing to do with me. It is their problem, after all, not mine, so why should I be depressed about it?

Stigma is a dangerous situation for one's health. I repeat, stigma can lead a person to commit suicide. And stigma is not just prejudice; for me, it is also lack of support and understanding in society. Stigma can be a signal for a person that "I am faulty," but for me, this is no longer the case; rather, it's more like "there is something wrong with the person for their prejudice!" In any case, it does not mean necessarily that I have to put up with people who are prejudiced. If I can help it, I get away from the stigma unless it is absolutely necessary that I cope with it."

Stella: "Anything else about the university experience?"

Alfredo: "No, not much. I mean, I did see a lot of problems, like the fact that many academics could not teach because they lacked the proper skills. They were mostly research fellows with little or no teaching skills. Those who could teach were very few, indeed. I also noticed that many academics disliked or resented students, often seeing them as a problem. That happens when academics do not have a passion for teaching. Being able to teach is a gift and, unfortunately, universities lack good teachers, which can cause all sorts of problems and internal tensions. All of these problems first made me depressed and then high. I became (hypo)manic and started to do a million things like painting, drawing, and music. I did anything but study.

In fact, my mind was no longer dedicated to the studies. I was wasting my time as if the university was not the right place for me. Indeed, the university is not the right place for me. It is too restrictive and I feel like my ideas are unwanted and I need to put them aside if I am to be part of tertiary studies. I felt that there was too much emphasis on science and research and not enough emphasis on humanitarian issues. Like the Dalai Lama writes, we need to integrate science with spirituality if we are to get close to real and complete knowledge. I needed people who cared, who were humanitarian, empathic, compassionate, creative. All I found were mostly cold and calculating academics with the exception of a few. And although these few academics tried to help me, it was a bit late by then because the (hypo)mania and the depression, given that I am a rapid cycler, had already become a problem."

Stella: "What do you mean when you say that you are a rapid cycler?"

Alfredo: "I could be depressed for a couple of weeks and then (hypo)manic for a week and then repeat the cycle. These were milder mood swings but, nevertheless, problematic. I can also have longer periods of (hypo)mania and depression and more severe symptoms."

Stella: "Who diagnosed you with Bipolar II, Alfredo?"

Alfredo: "It was Dr. Butler, my psychiatrist, who I still see occasionally because on the rare occasions when the (hypo)mania becomes troublesome, I need to take Epilim, which is Sodium Valproate, in small doses. That helps me to control the (hypo)mania. I usually stay on it two or three months of the year to avoid problems. But it is a small dose and I also help myself with natural methods. The mind can help tremendously and I am very familiar with "mindfulness," being an artist. I often lose myself when I create something. When I am (hypo)manic I can start many projects at once. I can paint, write poems, compose concertos, rock songs and write music in many different styles. I play the piano, fix computers, cook, and do many other things. It all happens at once and there is little sleep. Life is beautiful and there are so many things to do. Creativity just rushes in out of nowhere and the most incredible ideas come to mind. The feeling is all so beautiful.

It is like a natural drug that makes you feel good but there are dangers. Too little sleep and uncontrolled hypomania can lead to mania and that means detachment from reality, although, fortunately, that has never happened to me because my (hypo)mania does not turn into mania. My Bipolar is light and, as Stephen Fry writes, in America they call it Bipolar Light or Cyclothymia. But I feel that if I did not control myself, when (hypo)manic, it could get to that stage. Fortunately, I am a very responsible and careful person today; I am aware of my moods and when they change, and I have a set of strategies in place to help me. I have a strong support group of people who care for both me and my wife and who are all mental health professionals. Indeed, a support group is extremely important when we become affected by moods and symptoms."

Stella: "Let's go back to the time when you were burning your arms with the lit cigarette. What was happening in your mind then?"

Alfredo: "I was living in my car, a Valiant Regal sedan from 1969-1970, just outside Rozelle Mental Hospital. That car was my pride and joy. I had rebuilt the motor completely. I was gifted with mechanical things. Of course I did not know that my car was parked outside a psychiatric hospital. To me, the location was near a park so that it was convenient for me to live there for a while. It was the same area where I'd lived with my family for five years and there were lots of public toilets available. I was always fussy and even when homeless, I was clean; I washed myself well. Even the homeless people told me that I gave them a bad name because I was too clean for a homeless person. I did not smell much, at least not like them. The Obsessive Compulsive Disorder (OCD) made me into one of those extremely fussy people who clean themselves constantly; I had to wash my hands several times a day, and I mean up to thirty times. I would clean myself meticulously even without having a shower, and I did not worry about cold water; also, I had devised my own methods to wash myself well. Some of the homeless people really smelled terrible; yet I managed to communicate with them without letting them know that the smell was nearly suffocating me. I was a caring person; deep down, I cared for all people."

Stella: "And how long did you live in your car?"

Alfredo: "I lived in the car for approximately 3 to 4 weeks; I cannot remember exactly now. I had spent almost all of my money but I was not concerned. I think that I wanted to end my life somehow and I was trying to build up the courage to do so. I was killing myself by not eating. Too many things had gone wrong and my mother's death was the last straw that broke the camel's back."

[That was the end of the session for the week and I had a lot to think about. Talking about my past was giving me some perspective. It was helping me to see myself, to become self-critical. Inside, it felt like a storm was brewing, but a good storm, a storm that would help me to unload some heavy baggage. Even the fact that Stella is a fictional character is helping me. That is because Stella symbolizes my ability to engage in the self-therapeutic process and I feel that at some stage, we need to become so honest and critical with ourselves as to become our own therapists. This is what Stella represents most of all—my ability to do self-therapy and become my own psychologist, not in a complete sense because I will always need to go to therapy and seek the help of professionals, but to at least engage in some self-therapy so that I can benefit as much as possible from the therapeutic process.]

5 In Our Darkest Hour... We Start to See the Light

Stella: "How would you like to start this session Alfredo? Would you like to pick up from where we left off last week?"

Alfredo: "Yes, but where was I? I have so many things on my mind that I don't remember exactly where we left."

Stella: "We were talking about your experience as a homeless person and I asked you about the time when you were burning your arms with a lit cigarette."

Alfredo: "Ah yes, I remember. Fortunately, for me, a nurse, Sally, who was working in the hospital, saw me while I was burning my arms. I was in so much pain inside that I needed to feel physical pain to stop the inner torment. I think that this is what happens when young people inflict self-harm. They are in spiritual pain and need to translate this inner pain into physical pain, possibly to give it some visible expression, and in this sense, it could also be a cry for help. In fact, one of the worst things about mental disorders and anxiety or anguish is that no one can see anything. It is an internal suffering and because of this, a very lonely experience.

Self-harm is a complex issue and there are many reasons why people cause self-harm. It is also a visual ritual that gives visual meaning: the punishment of the body. I think it happens when people come to hate themselves. They finally turn the hate that they usually direct outwards, inwards—toward themselves. And it is this self-hate that often leads to suicide, I believe. In my opinion, self-harm is a sign of Post Traumatic Stress Disorder of substantial magnitude. Where would this self-hate come from? In my case, I remember my father's voice while he was telling me how bad I was, that I would never amount to much in life, that I was a mistake, and that I should never have been born. This kind of verbal abuse is very common in our Western world. During my cyber travels on the many websites I have visited, I have communicated with a large number of

Sally, the nurse
Drawing by Alfredo Zotti, 1982

This drawing is a strange sexless representation. She is a cheerful, kind person, not just a woman. Drawing by Alfredo Zotti, 1982

people who had been verbally abused in their childhood days. The abuse was constant and it could well be what negatively conditions people to come to believe that they are not good, that the reason why their life is so miserable is their fault."

Stella: "Would you tell me some more about Sally and how she approached you to help you?"

Alfredo: "The nurse knocked on the side window of the car. I was so malnourished and unwell that I could hardly see. For some incredible reason, she sat in the car next to me and I thought that that was unusual. I remember a funny thing: while I was malnourished and nearly dying, I still had the idea to put some perfume on because I liked to smell good. I had a bottle of Brut in my car, because it was one of the more affordable, pleasant and sophisticated aftershaves. Maybe this was a sign that I did not want to die, after all, and that deep inside, I had some very faint hope that things would work out for me.

She started to ask all sorts of questions and was now checking my pulse. She told me that I was probably very depressed and that I did not qualify for admission in the hospital. The hospital was for severely mentally ill patients. Nevertheless, she said, that because I was homeless and because I was so malnourished and I was causing self-harm, she could get me into the hospital, in the section where the less severe patients were, so that I could eat well for a while, get some antidepressants, and see a psychiatrist there. Mine were exceptional circumstances and I needed help from the hospital staff. She told me that I had to follow her to admission and that she was prepared to drag me there if she had to. I was so skinny and malnourished (I was just skin and bones) that she could have easily picked me up in her arms. She told me that I had penetrating brown eyes, the eyes of a special person. At that time, I did not see anything special about myself.

The nurse sent someone to get my car, which they left for me in the hospital's parking lot. She said that I was too weak and unwell to drive it myself. I was first taken to what today is known as the 'triage', where they took blood samples, my weight, and did various other tests. I was only 36 kilos (under 80 pounds), a walking skeleton for a man who is almost 170 cm (5' 7" tall and 23 years of age. After all the tests, I was taken to the main ward. I think that they gave me an antidepressant (it was a round, clear tablet with some greenish fluid in it, but I don't recall its name). I took my very first medication for depression. I had suffered with Bipolar II for many years without knowing about it. At times I felt that mood changes were part of everyone's experience of life. Deep down, however, I knew I was not completely normal. I felt that I was too sensitive and that I had special gifts.

The first few days, I mainly sat in the recreation room, waiting to eat while watching a bit of TV with the other patients. We were all medicated, some quite heavily. I had little energy and I was quite depressed. But the food was good and I finally had some good sleep. I could use the shower and the nice toilets, something that I had missed because of being homeless. For the first time, I felt that someone cared for me, that this was my new country now and that the government was giving me a chance to start again. I had no family because they had all gone back to Italy. I had no one. I was alone in Australia. A few good thoughts had started to form in my mind even though I was very depressed and, as the days went on, I felt that a huge dark cloud was beginning to lift from my shoulders.

The ward was huge and everything was connected: the eatery, the sleeping section upstairs, the psychiatrist's offices, and the recreation room. It took about three weeks for my severe depression to calm down.

I could go out for a walk, around the grounds of the hospital, which were right on the water, by the sea. No doubt it was a beautiful hospital, built in 1884. It was a historical site. The hospital comprised a number of buildings surrounded and enclosed by a huge wall, much like in the middle ages, when cities where surrounded by tall walls. There were many parks and recreational areas. It was quite vast. The catchment for the rain water was an underground engineering marvel. There was enough water stored there to satisfy a small town. And I thought to myself, "Some of the old technology was actually better than modern technology!" The buildings were beautiful and they captured my attention. Because I was already a visual artist, I started to draw sections of the buildings with pencils and charcoal. I still have the drawings with me and they are not too bad for a 23-year-old artist.

The patients there saw my drawings and they started to ask me questions about my visual art. There were quite a lot of artists amongst the patients there. We had singers, architects, musicians, and poets. No wonder that for the first time in my life, I felt that the environment and the people were really suitable to my personality. It was ironic that I found understanding amongst people with mental illness. Two things: either I was so mad that I could only function well amongst people with mental disorders or, alternatively, people with mental disorders were the truly sane people, for at least they were aware of their problems while so-called normal people were not. I tend to like the latter explanation. Why were there so many artists amongst those with mental disorders? This was an intriguing question. I was amongst artists, amongst people who are creative and sensitive and different. I was amongst caring people (the doctors and nurses) and life was beginning to smile at me again. Humanity was not all bad and there was still some hope for me. In the second part of the book, I include Chapter 14, titled "Creative People and Mental Disorders" on page 121.

Unbelievable as it sounds, in the hospital, I found some of the most compassionate people, and I felt good; I felt that someone cared for me. I also loved the patients and found that they were very creative, compassionate and kind. These were people who had suffered terrible traumas and who needed help. I shared many stories with the patients there, and I even wrote some of their stories in my diary. There was not a single patient who had not experienced childhood trauma, with the great majority having been sexually abused. These were my kind of people. I was in the hospital for two months and there I had the best time of my life, although there was plenty of sadness as well, particularly when a patient needed to be physically restrained and controlled because of experiencing an episode of psychosis."

Stella: "How did you feel when you saw a patient being restrained?"

Alfredo: "I knew that it was necessary, but I wonder if it is possible to calm the patient down without need for physical restraint. I have had some experiences with psychotic people, who had become violent, and I found that I had some gift that I could use to calm them down. This is possibly because I had to control my alcoholic father, sometimes. Actually, if it was not for my ability to defuse situations, in some rare and intense situations, there was a chance that my father could have become physically violent toward my mother and us children. I was always able to calm things down. Perhaps it is this that has helped me later to calm people who suffer with psychosis. And the funny thing is that many people with psychosis were going to cross my path in my lifetime—twice while living in a government complex, and six times while working as a volunteer cook in a shelter for homeless people."

Stella: "Can you give me an example of how you have defused situations?"

Alfredo: "I can tell you the story of Boris, who was in the hospital with me.

Boris was a Russian migrant who had been admitted to Rozelle Hospital five days before my arrival. In fact, in the afternoon on my first day, I had seen Boris taken to the padded room in a straightjacket by two security nurses because he had an attack of psychosis and had become agitated and violent. It had taken about a couple of weeks to stabilize Boris and I was pleased to see him peaceful and relaxed.

While many patients there probably became stressed to see Boris taken away to the padded room, I was accustomed to all the drama because of my father's alcoholism. My father would often carry on in a silly way, break furniture and start all sorts of tantrums. In his very drunken and agitated state, he was not that different from someone experiencing psychosis. But while Boris had schizophrenia, my father was an alcoholic. To me, it was not something new to see someone in distress. So I told Boris that next time he felt like he was going to lose control, he might come to me and I would help him. He did, and when this happened, I took him for a walk; we would walk for a long time and then sit quietly somewhere and do some breathing exercises. But I feel that it was my friendship that truly helped him, my presence as a friend. After that, he no longer had attacks where he needed to be restrained and even the doctors wondered what had made the difference. Of course, I did not tell them because they would not believe that a friendship could help a sufferer to control his psychotic attacks. But I believe it.

I started to talk to Boris and we soon became good friends. He clearly had visible scars on his skull because he had shaved all his hair. He had been attacked by a street gang while experiencing episodes of psychosis. Unfortunately, this is what often happens to people with mental illness because society does not understand, and we have no means of assisting someone in mental distress, nor any education to know the difference between someone who is experiencing psychosis and someone who is just a troublemaker, drunk, on drugs, or whatever. I can tell the difference.

Boris asked me why was it that I talked to him and that I was his friend. After all, he could be violent, he told me. I said to Boris that I was not afraid of him and that he would never be violent toward me. 'How do you know?' Boris asked. I replied, 'Because I think that I have a gift with people who suffer like you and that is, to not be afraid and to be open and transparent so that people like you get to trust me.' Boris looked at me and smiled. He felt safe around me and this is what made the difference. I accepted him and was not afraid.

While I was not sure at the time if my hunch of being able to calm people with psychosis was true—it was just a feeling then—I know today that it is absolutely true. Many times, in my attempt to help homeless people as a volunteer, I have come across people with schizophrenia, who could have been violent and some who were experiencing psychosis.

I've also lived in a government complex of houses where some neighbors suffered with schizophrenia. But I feel that because I do have a special gift, I was always able to defuse dangerous situations. I do believe that people who know how to handle people with psychosis are always pretty safe. I mean, you don't get into arguments with someone who is having psychosis. You agree with them and do your best to make them feel at ease. In such moments, one has to focus on the person who is having psychosis and do the best to assist the person. This is not the time for arguments, but for understanding and compassion.

For example, I was once in a car with someone with schizophrenia, who had a psychotic attack. Fortunately, he safely stopped the car and started screaming and banging his hands on the steering wheel. I sat there calmly and when I had a chance, I spoke to him calmly. When he turned and looked at me, as if he was going to attack me, I grabbed his arms and told him that everything would be fine, to try and calm down, that we would go for a walk and get some fresh air. We got out of the car and went for a walk. I had no idea that this musician had schizophrenia, let alone that he had severe psychosis. But I was fortunate to sense immediately that he had a mental disorder. We were just playing music in a band at the time. But I was able to handle him and things turned out well.

Of course, I was also fortunate. In some rare cases, people with psychosis can turn violent; but I was fortunate to be able to defuse the situation. Maybe it's luck; but I have a hunch that what we do in these situations is also very important and there should be more education in society about it. I was always able to defuse situations like this and sufferers always liked me and respected me. Some people have this gift and that is why later in life, I decided that I could truly help people with mental disorders, even serious cases. Little did I know that I was going to marry a beautiful lady who suffers with Bipolar I Disorder. In the initial stages, my wife did have some psychosis and again, it was my gift that helped me to help her. Today she is stable, although she has other disabilities, as well.

Boris and I remained good friends throughout my stay at Rozelle Hospital and when the time to leave came, I remember that Boris disappeared for a couple of days till I went to find him and we had a good, long talk. Generally, people could not understand why I was so friendly with a dangerous psychotic patient. But to me, Boris was harmless; he was just someone who needed help, someone who needed to be trusted and helped. And I gave him trust, even though I only knew this subconsciously, for I had no clear knowledge of any of this. But I often went with my heart and let it guide me. I told Boris that I would come to visit and that I would not just disappear. This was a comfort to him."

Stella: "Very interesting, Alfredo, and I really think that you do have a gift with people which, as you say, you could have developed when you had to calm your father down. But you are also a very empathetic person. Maybe you understand that a psychotic attack is a cry for help and that these troubled people are afraid and possibly need someone to help them, someone they can trust."

Alfredo: "Yes, Stella, you could be right. There were some nurses at Rozelle Hospital who also had a gift with patients and could calm them down.

The mental health professionals of Rozelle Hospital were truly advanced in those days and I have nothing but respect for these wonderful people, because they laid the foundation for the mental health care that we have today in Australia. It was a wonderful experience. The funny thing is that my psychiatrist, Dr. Butler, who I see once every couple of months, also worked at Rozelle while he was in training in psychiatry, although we never met while I was there. What I am trying to say is that this hospital was a place where mental health professionals went to learn, to learn from the school of life. Today, unfortunately, the hospital is no longer there. Art and creativity were quite important at the time. There were plenty of opportunities to sing, play, draw, or engage in creative activities. Many patients belonged to their own group of people who were writers, poets, scientists, visual artists, or singers. I belonged to quite a few groups, given my various talents. I started to play the piano daily for the people who loved the music there."

Stella: "Tell me about the hospital, Alfredo. What was it like?"

Alfredo: "The grounds of Rozelle Hospital were an inspiration to an artist like me. The surrounding landscape and the beautiful buildings set the whole space apart, as if it were in another space and time. I've written a poem about it."

Stella: "How does the poem go? Would you like to share it with me?"

Alfredo: "Of course...."

Rozelle Hospital

The land lies calmly.
It is protected
from the irrationality of the world
as if in another space and time.
Amongst the trees and the bird calls those of us who are here
are left to contemplate.
Where is the wisdom?
Where is the love?
That through the centuries should have blossomed to shape
the finest heart?
Nowhere in sight.
We look at the land that now seems to have given up and no
longer waits."

Stella: "You know it by heart?"

Alfredo: "Yes, Stella, most creative things I do I know by heart.

For me, Rozelle Hospital was a magnificent place and this is how I perceived it to be, though every individual would have a different experience. But I don't know any patients who hated it. Most said that they were protected from the outside world that for us, ironically, was a crazy world.

My experience was positive. This was partly because on the third day, the placebo effect of the antidepressants had kicked in. But I also felt that I had been taken away from what I perceived to be a 'crazy' world. I was now in a pleasant environment where people were trying to help me. Many patients there were trying to find their way in the world; they were trying to cope with their disabilities. This was an environment of compassion, love, and understanding, not one of greed, selfishness and corruption.

It is true that there were patients who had severe schizophrenia and could be dangerous. The population of the inpatients also included some who had paranoid delusions and who saw enemies everywhere. True that they were medicated, but they could become agitated at any moment and it was quite possible for them to have a relapse, even if medicated. I never felt any danger and for this, I was well-loved by all the patients there.

These people never behaved in any hostile manner toward me. I think they really liked me because I was honest with them, whenever I could be, and treated them with respect. I think that they sensed that I was a friend, not someone who would judge them in any way. In their own words, they saw me as an ally rather than an enemy. The local psychiatrist told me that I had a special gift with the patients. It was at that moment that I felt that my future would have to be one where I help people with mental disorders. I understood them well and I could really help these people. At the time, I lacked knowledge of mental disorders and I was inexperienced, but I decided that I would study one day and become a helper for these special people who had been so traumatized. I heard their stories.

There was not one patient who had not been repeatedly and severely traumatized during their childhood days. [I know this because I am reading entries from my journal I wrote while I was at the hospital with all sorts of information, including the patients' history and disorders. Later, I was to make a lot of sense of this, especially after becoming a friend of counseling psychologist Dr. Bob Rich, who still helps me with my personal research on childhood trauma. I have written an essay, included in the second part of this book, titled "Childhood Trauma."]

On the grounds of this beautiful hospital, I had not felt this good in a very long time. I belonged to this place and to these people. I had problems and not only could I speak about the problems, but people were listening with interest. This was unusual, given that I had strong ethnic looks—black hair and olive skin—and a strong accent. But this did not matter, for what was required was that there be honesty and to have a heart. In this hospital, stigma was almost nonexistent. This was the main factor that helped my recovery. This is why I believe that we need advanced centers for mental health, similar to institutions, but where the focus is on recovery. We'll explore this idea more in part II of this book.

In my first week at the hospital, I was able to walk on the grounds and I made some of my best drawings there. I have kept the drawings to this day, along with this diary that I am now editing to make this short book.

After breakfast, on the third day, I decided to explore the grounds of the hospital. I had asked for permission to go out to draw some sketches of some of the buildings there.

It was the Colonial government who had bought the site comprising 105 acres and, with remarkable foresight, anticipated that many convicts and migrants would need some sort of institutionalization. The asylum was designed according to the principles of Dr. Thomas Kirkbride. James Barrett, who was a Colonial Architect of the times, designed the buildings. He worked in collaboration with Inspector of the Insane, Dr. Fredrick Norton Manning. The complex of buildings was completed in 1885 and subsequently named the Kirkbride Block, offering progressive patient care. Together, they produced a group of twenty neo-classical buildings made of sandstone, following a style known as Victorian Italianate.

The buildings did remind me of Italy, my home country. In particular, I had fallen in love with the Venetian Clock Tower that had a metallic sphere on top, which rose and fell according to the water level of the reservoir that could contain thousands of liters of rainwater, running underneath much of the hospital grounds, enough to provide for the needs of the hospital, which housed hundreds of people."

Stella: "You really liked the old buildings and the natural setting of the hospital?"

Alfredo: "Yes, I did, Stella, and I also liked the people there. I was aware that unless I helped myself, I could not help others and that I also lacked knowledge of mental illness. But true to my word, I studied mental disorders and began to help people later. The people I most loved were the people who suffered like me, and also some (unfortunately, not all) mental health professionals, like psychologists, psychiatrists, and nurses. These were, and still are, my kind of people, people with a heart."

Rozelle Hospital's main entrance
Drawing by Alfredo Zotti, 1982

The Venetian Tower at Rozelle Hospital
Drawing by Alfredo Zotti, 1982

Stella: "I am afraid that we have come to the end of this session, Alfredo. We will continue next week. Thank you for sharing so much of yourself and your story, Alfredo. I really appreciate it."

Alfredo: "Thank you, Stella, see you next week."

6 "We'll meet again, don't know where, don't know when..."

The car drive to Stella's practice was very inspiring. It was a beautiful sunny day and Terrigal (New South Wales) is a wonderful place on a sunny day. I decided to take some photos of the beach before going to my therapy session so that I arrived at Terrigal a couple of hours before the appointment. I love taking photos with my digital camera. When I get home, I usually touch the photos up with Adobe Photoshop. The time went really quickly so that I headed for the clinic, which was on the first floor. It was an old house remodeled into a therapy studio. When I got there, I sat in the waiting room.

Stella: "Hi, Alfredo, come in and tell me what has been happening lately."

Alfredo: "This time I do remember the exact spot where we left off. I will pick up the story from there. I had noticed the upright piano in the recreation room of the hospital, but never attempted to play it until I built up enough courage. I was very shy until I got to know the people; but once the ice had been broken, my shyness would turn into confidence. My shyness was due to all of the problems, the traumas, and mostly due to my father's alcoholism and disapproval of me. I had lost confidence. I had experienced very stressful situations."

Stella: "You have, indeed, had a traumatic life, Alfredo, but an interesting one. I feel that the reason why you are such a creative, compassionate and helpful person today is partly because of the trauma that you have experienced and because you have been able to survive it. What does not break you makes you stronger. And just the attempt to cope with so many problems requires great creativity and the ability to find a way out, so to speak. When did you start playing the piano in the hospital?"

Alfredo: "It was one afternoon before the medication bell went off. There was not a single person in the recreation room, so I opened the lid and started to play quietly, engaging the damper pedal. The piano was a

Bosendorfer (a sign that Australia was indeed an affluent country, for this was one of the best pianos ever made, second to the Steinway). I was playing *We'll Meet Again*, an old song that my mother really liked and sang quite often. Since she had passed away, I hoped that the sound would reach her in the sky. I was playing to her with such feeling that a patient who had sneaked in became teary-eyed. Soon a few others came in and a couple of older ladies started to sing: "We'll meet again, don't know when, don't know where, but I know we'll meet again some sunny day..." and so it went. Many people were now singing and I had to accompany them; I could not stop even though I had suddenly become shy and the music was now uncertain. But I had an entire choir behind me, a beautiful choir. I closed my eyes and went for it. The piano suddenly had gained a full sound and now it was more like an orchestra, not just a piano.

The next song I played was *As Time Goes By*. And we kept playing and singing until we heard the bell go off, signaling that it was time for our medication. They kept singing that same song some twenty times or so. It was good, however, because that was a kind of music therapy.

From that day, some of the patients demanded that I play the piano each day. They were quite good singers, in perfect tune. To be honest, I wish that some of the professionals would sing that way, as the patients did, from the heart. From that day, I learned the power of music in therapy, because all of us began to feel so much better with the music sessions. Singing and playing music was a tremendous boost to our spirit. It was wonderful. I even began to play some jazz like Gershwin and music was now the talk of the ward. I was a famous patient, an artist, and the patients there really liked me, although some, as usual, saw my talent as threatening and as a way to show off.

The doctors and nurses loved the music and my resident psychiatrist gave me a book titled *Music Therapy* (1966) by Juliette Alvin, which I still have today, signed by the psychiatrist. There was a nurse who I think was developing feelings for me, as I was for her. She was beautiful and very kind. She would join in the singing, as well. But I was a patient and she was working there so that, unfortunately, nothing further ever eventuated.

The local psychiatrist looked into my eyes and said, "You're a special person, Alfredo; don't waste your talents; put them to good use to help others." He knew that my music was therapeutic and not commercial. The harmonies and the melodies were perfect for healing. Today, I still write and compose therapeutic music. Honestly speaking, most of what I do today is because of my experiences at Rozelle Hospital. What a wonderful place and evidence that deinstitutionalization is not always a good thing!

I would not be here if it weren't for the staff of Rozelle Hospital. No doubt that I would have taken my life. Not only did they save my life, but they helped me become a better person, showing me my life's path. The psychiatrist was brilliant, a rare man with many years of experience. The knowledge I got there did not help me immediately, but as the years have gone by, and I have had a chance to reflect on the experiences there, I can say with certainty that Rozelle gave me the foundations that enabled me to build a better life for myself. They gave me hope, supported me, and made me aware that there are good and caring people out there and that not all people are prejudiced.

There I learned that I could be an artist without being famous and that being an artist to help people was much more rewarding than to be an artist who tries to make as much money as possible, someone who seeks fame and fortune alone. I have nothing against those who make it in life, but that is not what I was about. The heart and the spirit were the most important things for me, not money or possessions. My heart had to be in it for my creativity to flourish. Money and fame were of secondary importance and not a necessity.

After two months, I started to feel a bit high, for the [hypo]mania was setting in, most likely due to the antidepressants. Because I was so terribly depressed, it had taken quite a while for the tablets to work a little, although I feel that most of it was placebo, plus the fact that I was now much happier. But my [hypo]mania has never turned into full-blown mania so that with the positive frame of mind I was in, the psychiatrist (not knowing I suffered with Bipolar II) told me that I could start to look for work and that he would leave instructions for the hospital staff to let me in the ward so long as it was before six at night.

I was free to go out and search for work, and I found it. I also found a little room to live in. I was able to sleep and eat at the hospital for a while till I made enough money to put a deposit on the little room, at that time in Annandale, Sydney, which was near the hospital. The psychiatrist had been very kind in that way, letting me stay till I had enough money to go my own way. That was an experience in itself. Of course the patients became extremely sad that I was leaving the hospital so soon. What about the music afternoons? I promised the patients that I would come back every Sunday and that we would have our music afternoon then. I would not abandon them. The psychiatrist agreed and I was able to come to visit the patients and play with them for quite a long while."

Stella: "Where did you find work?"

Alfredo: "The work I found was as an organ player in a bar/restaurant in Kings' Cross, called the Vienna Inn, which was open all night. My life was to suddenly improve and I was to meet my wife, Cheryl, who was a beautiful woman with blue eyes, soft light skin, and wonderful and long brownish/red hair. She was so beautiful that she had a few offers to work as a model but never took them up, because she suffered with Bipolar I, a very serious condition. The strangest of things is that when we met, we both had just been discharged from different psychiatric hospitals: I was just out of Rozelle, while my wife had just been released from St. Vincent's Hospital. What are the chances of this happening? It does sound unbelievable, but true. There is documentation for this; it isn't something I am making up. My wife and I have a special understanding and we have been looking after each other and our mental disorder ever since we met. We are soulmates and perfect for each other because we understand our personalities and our mental disorder perfectly. My wife is 9 years older than I am. As I write this, I am in my mid-50s and she is in her mid-60s, but our love for each other is still the same. As the years go by, the relationship is not just about sex, but it has become much more important. It becomes pure love and friendship, a kind of spiritual love that keeps us warm and gives us a sense of safety in a world that is highly unpredictable."

Stella: "Alfredo, this is a wonderful story and I'm sure that one day you'll write it down to inspire others and to show your strength, resilience, and love in spite of the presence of a very serious mental disorder. How did you calm down your [hypo]mania? Did you take something for it?"

Alfredo: "I am not proud of it, Stella, because I used recreational drugs and alcohol. I don't know how I managed, but I feel that when I came out of the hospital, the mania was not that troublesome yet. I was 23 years of age. The mania suddenly became very troublesome when I reached about 30 years of age. I did smoke pot, though, not a real lot but I did use it, and drank alcohol quite often. These days I don't smoke or drink anything and haven't done so for about 20 years. I don't drink or smoke, not even cigarettes. However, I never smoked or drank so abusively for that to be a problem. I could always stop myself when I had had enough."

Stella: "Yes, I agree, Alfredo, it's because there is no substance abuse in your history that you are doing reasonably well today. Your condition is serious, but you can cope because you take care of yourself so well. You want help and you let others help you; and if you make a mistake or your behavior changes, you are aware of it, and you always apologize to people for it. I think that this is something to admire because being aware is important.

So, tell me of your new job as an organ player."

Alfredo: "When I arrived at the Old Vienna Inn to apply for the job, I immediately noticed a huge Hammond organ with lots of buttons and switches and a very extensive bass pedal board. The manager said: 'The organist left us because we were truly sick of his classical music. We told him we'd no longer tolerate Bach, especially the more agitated pieces, and that we just wanted some easy listening music, kind of New Age, to calm the troubled souls that come here to find some peace. He took offence to that and told me he'd quit the job. He asked for his last paycheck and off he went!'

Billy was the name of the manager, so I told him that New Age was my kind of music and that my music was all about therapy, calming people down when needed, and making people laugh or dance when this was required. 'The only problem,' I said to Bill, 'is that I've never played an organ, so I may need to practice for a few hours to learn how to operate the Hammond.' 'No problem,' said Bill. 'Come tomorrow morning at about 7 AM. You can practice until 9 AM. That is the best time to practice.' I agreed and got there 10 minutes before 7 the next day.

I sat at the organ, after Bill had made a nice coffee for me that came with a biscuit, and I switched on the enormous organ. It had two keyboards and the pedal board, and it was a B3 Hammond with some extra buttons, because this was a special edition of that model. It didn't take me long to learn to play the bass with my right foot, and the keyboard with the two hands. I felt a bit like an octopus with all the four limbs busy doing something: the right leg was controlling the volume pedal; the left leg was controlling the bass pedal; the left hand was playing that bottom keyboard; and the right hand was playing the top keyboard. I was playing *Just the Thought of You*.

Billy was a New Zealand Maori man in his 40s, tall and well-dressed with a white shirt and his black vest. A very stylish man and he had a heart of gold. He came to me with a big smile, saying that I was perfect for the job and he was extremely happy to have me. The music that came out of that organ was incredible even to me. The Hammond organ was truly wonderful and sounded like a big orchestra, a jazz orchestra. I was playing all the old standards, like *Raindrops, My Way, As Time Goes By*, and many of the movie themes.

Very soon, musicians came to visit me in after hours because I was playing well into the small hours of the night. There were famous musicians like Mark Hunter of *Dragons* and Paul Hester of *Crowded House*, who often went to the Menzil Room, a rock night club that was just a few doors from me. Sometimes I did the same and went to the Paradise Room after I had finished for the night, where people like James Morrison were playing. I had the pleasure of playing a few tunes with the then young James Morrison and his band, but I also jammed with other famous people."

Stella: "It must have been difficult for you to be surrounded by famous people, to play with them, and yet not being able to become famous yourself? Was this frustrating for you?"

Alfredo: "It is not easy to answer this question, Stella. I think that deep down, we all want to be recognized; it's only human nature. But I feel that my real purpose in this life is to achieve something different, not fame. I feel that I am doing what I need to do and I only have to answer to God, not to anyone else. In this sense, my kind of voluntary work is more important, I feel, than becoming famous or rich. Don't think I envy that kind of life, which can be often meaningless and a narrow-minded lifestyle.

I am writing journals today, together with other people who suffer with a mental disorder, and these journals are travelling all over the world, reaching people everywhere, and it's all possible thanks to the technology, the computer. Many health professionals are reading my journal, the *Anti Stigma Crusaders Journal,* and they are noticing that the real experience of sufferers is quite different from the knowledge available in books. Mental disorders are not something that can be understood from reading books alone. We need to understand their real-life experiences if we are to actually help people."

Stella: "Yes, I agree, Alfredo. We do need to study the experiences of sufferers and that's why I hope that in the future there will be more sufferers amongst the mental health professionals, like you."

Alfredo: "Yes, Stella, that is why I am studying psychology at university."

Stella: "Please, continue with your story."

Alfredo: "Yes, sure, Stella...

I had a reasonably good job and I was happy. It was in that period that I met my wife, who at that time was the drink manager of the well-known Manzil Room, a famous nightclub, just a couple of doors down from where I played. It all started one night when Cheryl came into the Old Vienna Inn and sat at a table. She is still beautiful today, but now we are older, so it is a little different. In those days, she was younger and a stunning looking young woman.

She listened to my music with great interest and kept coming on and off for the next two weeks. One night she came to the organ as I was playing "Stardust" and told me that she felt I was a special person and that she'd like to talk to me and have coffee somewhere if possible. My music had touched her in some way. I told her that I would love to have coffee with her the next day. As it turned out, it was her day off. We went to a nearby coffee shop where the coffee aroma was truly out of this world. We fell in love and that was the beginning of our life together.

Impression of Cheryl, my wife

We're still together and still much in love after thirty-three years.

We didn't know at that time that I suffered with Bipolar II and that she suffered with Bipolar I. We soon found out when things went wrong. My wife lost her consciousness for two weeks because of mania that could not be controlled. We were not on medication and had no idea of what mania really was. But as the doctor told us, it is not uncommon for the mania to intensify or show up at around 30 years of age.

My (hypo)mania came when I turned 30. I'd had a little of it all of my life, but nothing of the intensity that I experienced in my 30s. I don't want to go into what mania is and what my wife and I experienced, for it's too terrible to go back to those days. It was painful, frightening, and troublesome for us. But what's important is that we survived and that we have been able to save our marriage. God only knows how we managed to survive it all. In fact, it was our marriage that saved us. Today, no mania would be powerful enough to unsettle us. We can cope and we can control it before it gets the better of us. We have used everything possible to stay well and we find that if we look after ourselves, we can cope very well, and have a reasonably normal life. Perhaps it is because we both suffer with bipolar that we have been able to forgive and tolerate each other. Many other couples have broken up over such things, but we have made the best of it, and it has paid off.

As the years went by, it became clear that my wife could no longer hold a full-time job and that her physical condition was deteriorating. She had attempted suicide twice while we were married.

Once I was playing at a night club and when I returned home, I found my wife shaking, sweating, and almost unconscious. She had taken an overdose of Mellaril (Thioridazine), which was a drug for schizophrenia. Unfortunately, her first psychiatrist had mistaken her condition for schizophrenia and put her on these drugs that were unsuitable and possibly the reason why she attempted suicide.

I lifted my wife up in my arms and carried her to the car. I rushed her to St. Vincent's Hospital, where she was immediately taken in. Fortunately, she recovered well and the next day I went to pick her up. My wife said, 'I suppose that you are going to leave me now?' 'I am not going to leave you,' I said. 'You're my wife and we are stuck with each other. But there is one thing we have to discuss, though—when you feel better, that is. Not for now.'

In the next two days, I made her promise that she would never do anything like that because if I did that to her, how would she feel? I think that she understood and has never attempted suicide again. I am quite certain that today she would never do anything of the sort."

Stella: "And what about you, Alfredo? Have there been any suicide attempts in your life?"

Alfredo: "Yes, once I did try and took an overdose of potent medication. I was taken to hospital and resuscitated. But it was a miracle because I was clinically dead for a while. I had a wonderful experience, like many others, of going into the tunnel of Light. But this was my second time into the tunnel. The first time was years back when I was only 10 and was hit by a car. I nearly died at that time, too, and it was a miracle that I was brought back.

I don't want to go into it in detail, but when I arrived near the end of the tunnel, on both occasions, a voice told me that it was not my time and that I should go back. "Go back to what?" I said. A voice told me that my life was not over yet and that I had two choices: either go back and finish my life or go further into the tunnel, be reborn, and go through another life on Earth. The choice was mine. I understood that the sensible thing to do was to go back. So I went back and that is why I lived, I believe. From that day, the second time I experienced the tunnel of Light, I became truly spiritual and I do like the idea of God, though God, for me, is not a person but more the universe and consciousness."

Stella: "Your story is truly a wonderful story of determination, love, and compassion. I am very touched by it, Alfredo, and I'm glad that you have decided to write a short book about it; it will surely help many sufferers out there."

Alfredo: "Thank you, Stella, but I must give a lot of credit to psychologist Dr. Bob Rich for his kindness, my psychiatrist, Dr. Butler, for his wisdom, and recently, my psychologist, Paul Corcoran, who helps me and my wife to cope with our work of helping many sufferers online. Bob Rich, in particular, has helped me understand that what we call mental illness is nothing more or less than a kind of suffering or anguish that rises either from traumatic experiences or from the creative process, coupled with a genetic weakness. With the help of these mental health professionals, I was able to gain the right knowledge that has brought me here today. There are many other people who have supported me and helped me through my journey. Dr. Dean Cavanagh, our family doctor who specializes in mental illness has supported my wife and me for many years. Professor Trevor Waring, of the University of Newcastle, is one of these people. Although I have known him for a short time, his advice and feedback have been tremendously helpful. And there have been others that have been kind and supportive, like Professor Pat McGorry."

Stella: "Yes, I tend to agree, Alfredo. There have been tremendous changes in you in the past two or three years. It's very possible that through both your hard work and the support of your mental health professional friends, you have developed the ability to see so deeply into your condition and this has had very positive outcomes because to really look at oneself with honesty, and in terms of our place in the wider social setting, is something rare and wonderful. I think that we are at the end of our session, Alfredo."

Alfredo: "Yes, Stella, we have gone well over the hour now. Thank you. I feel much better. You must have really been interested in what I was saying."

Stella: "Yes, I have, Alfredo. Thank you for your honesty. Your wife is right when she says that you are a special man, difficult to understand but special, nevertheless. You have many gifts which you use to help others. I'll see you next week."

As I went out of the room, I was thinking about how art was a huge part of my life; and now that I look back at all of this, I tend to think that being sensitive, creative, and different, unless we become famous, may not be ideal for society. Why is it OK for famous people to have a mental illness, to be different, and to be creative and not for ordinary people? What is going on? Too many thoughts ran through my mind and, to be honest, I came to understand that a diagnosis of mental disorder depends not only on the behavior, personality, or biological and genetic nature of a person, but also on the person's status, cultural background, intelligence, ideas, and much more. A mental disorder is such a complex thing that in many ways, we are also creating mental disorders where there aren't any. Do I suffer with a mental disorder? Or am I just sensitive, creative, and different? Or perhaps, is it the trauma that is my real problem? I don't know with certainty, but I hope that my story serves to make me think, so that I can better understand what's going on.

The idea of Stella has served me well. She is a figment of my imagination, a character that I have created to give my spirit and consciousness a name. I do believe that there is a separate spirit that is part of every human being, something with which many academics and intellectuals would disagree. Why? I feel that many academics and intellectuals have a very developed left side of the brain, but an under-developed right side. I feel that both sides of my brain are equally developed and from experience, I know that sufferers with mental disorders, who are able get in touch with their spirit, often learn to watch themselves from a distance. No matter how complex the brain is, it is difficult for me to believe that the brain can watch over itself without the aid of the spirit. Because having the ability to watch over oneself requires intuition, some premonition, and the ability to sense one's environment. I am still learning to do this and I sense that it is my spirit that makes it possible for me to watch my distorted thoughts, my moods, and various symptoms. Some call it the mind watching over the mind; but I prefer to say that it's the spirit watching over the mind.

PART II:
Treatment and Critique

7 | Spirituality and Coping with Mental Illness

Remember the initial question that I had posed myself? "What is a mental disorder, or mental illness, as some prefer to call it?" Some important things have begun to surface, so that I feel quite confident now in attempting to answer the question. In my mind, there is no doubt that it is not an illness like any other, and in fact, the word illness is wrongly used to define this particular kind of human suffering. For one thing, the brain is plastic and it can readjust itself. It is unlike any other organ. However, we must not overestimate the plasticity of the brain because change, after years of suffering with a mental disorder, is very difficult to achieve. We are well aware that a suitable environment and social support do wonders in helping sufferers to either learn to cope or recover. Recovery is mostly seen in younger clients, especially through early interventions. While full recovery is possible in some cases, sufferers with chronic mental disorders, who have experienced the disorder for many years, have to resign themselves to the fact that the only possibility is to learn to cope with their mental disorder, which will be with them for life. This is certainly my case.

Three things have really helped my wife and me: spirituality, creativity, and knowledge. Spirituality and creativity have helped us to face very difficult times that, without spiritual, belief can be overwhelming and often lead to suicide. I will explore these issues in the essays that I have included here, which I believe are pertinent to this discussion. But before I begin with the various essays, I would like to briefly state that spirituality can be tremendously helpful, as part of the therapy. But what do I mean by the term "spirituality"? By spirituality, I don't mean anything to do with specific religions, but rather to do with that part of being human that cannot be explained in scientific and/or rational terms. The Royal College of Psychologists (RC PSYCH, 2012) gives us the following definition, which I feel is appropriate for this discussion:

Spirituality involves experiences of:
- a deep-seated sense of meaning and purpose in life;
- a sense of belonging;
- a sense of connection of 'the deeply personal with the universal';
- acceptance, integration, and a sense of wholeness.

What is important to state is that spirituality is different from religion because it is not tied to any religious belief. My friend Judy explains it as follows:

> ...Even though I used to be a very strong church-going person, I wouldn't say that I had much spirituality. I believe that my working to manage my depression has unfolded my true spirituality and I think what it is, is that it gives a sense of purpose to my life and an understanding that we are just a small part of the universal collective, or the world. If we heal ourselves, we start to heal the world. Sometimes it feels like it's probably at the pace of one grain of sand at a time on a beach, but nevertheless, it makes a difference. Sometimes it helps me to stand back, apart from the depression, and see that there are bigger things going on and the universe is not out to "get" me, which can be a common feeling with depression. It is hard to describe, for sure. My therapist is a very spiritual person, which has been a very important factor in my healing, as well.

Physical and mental states also have an impact on mental illness. For example, there are serious problems with our Western life, a life that is mostly driven by greed, competition, selfishness, and lots of mental activities. In many ways, we do lead a mental life where the mind leads the body. I am here talking about the pervasive forces of ideology. And speaking of ideology, one of the most powerful is the ideology that medication can help or even cure people with mental disorder. Is this so? The reality is that medication, especially if combined with therapy, can be very helpful. Therapy, however, is the most important in my eyes because it often leads the sufferer to develop methods that can be used for long-term maintenance that are not always possible, or as efficient, in pharmacotherapy alone.

Research tends to indicate that antidepressants do not work well, especially in long-term treatment. Double-blind studies indicate that antidepressants are not much better than placebos, and antipsychotics have little or no success in long-term treatment. Antipsychotics can help some people who suffer with psychosis, and in some situations can even save lives, but the long-term treatment is often unsuccessful because of the severity of side effects and because these drugs tend to lose efficacy so that bigger does or alternative medications are needed. Anticonvulsants have a better track record and are used as preventative maintenance.

For example, people who suffer with bipolar often do benefit from Epilim (Sodium Valproate) or Lithium, and Epilim is also used to control schizophrenia. These two anticonvulsants are the most effective of all medication because they can reduce the severity of moods and help sufferers to live a more normal life. Why do they work so well in people who can tolerate the side effects? This remains unknown. Lithium is a very old drug discovered by an Australian doctor, John Cade, back in the 1940s. Lithium, in Bipolar Disorder, can help areas of the brain that are affected by the disorder to repair themselves. For example, early childhood abuse can result in the decrease in size of areas of the brain involved in emotion regulation and studies have shown that it may protect neurons from damage. Differences between patients taking Lithium and those who do not may be due to this. Lithium also acts like a modulator for neural impulses.

But Lithium and Epilim are anticonvulsants that are used by more responsible psychiatrists and doctors, because there is pressure, and often rewards to prescribe more modern antipsychotics dugs. Indeed, while these drugs cannot be tolerated by every sufferer with bipolar, they are known to be effective for a wide population. Antipsychotics do not have a good long-term track record. For these reasons, it is important to consider alternative interventions and natural therapy to combine with medication and hence the claim that bio-psychosocial methods are the best. And also that medication is used as a kind of temporary intervention until the patient is stabilized and given a chance to use more natural ways to control his/her disorder and learn some coping strategies. If the medication is needed permanently, then additional methods such as exercise, good nutrition, knowledge, meditation, mindfulness, and reasonably stress-free life will all help the sufferer to rely on less medication or a lower dose. Today I use Epilim to help myself but not all the time. I use it three or four months of the year when the (hypo)mania becomes troublesome. I can cope with depression and do not take antidepressants for it, but (hypo)mania is a much more difficult state of mind to control.

In my opinion, spirituality can be tremendously helpful as part of the therapy.

I have identified three major characteristics which contribute to the great bulk of what we call mental illness, and in my opinion, improving these areas of social interaction and culture would lead to a dramatic reduction of serious mental disorders and especially stigma. These are:

(a) capitalism, which is a problematic social system based on greed, competition, myths and ideology, and disregard for the human condition and related human nature, which is unsupportive to sufferers. These characteristics of our corporate world make it possible for stigma to thrive. Stigma is the negative perception society holds and maintains through media, but also a straying from the norm. The perspective is also known and internalized by the sufferer and a norm by which he or she may make self-judgments. Of course some symptoms may arise from this;

(b) childhood traumas and traumatic experiences; and

(c) our failure to value and understand the complexities of a creative and sensitive mind that cannot appropriately express itself in a capitalist society and that we tend to define as genetic deficiency.

By attending to these three factors, we could drastically reduce mental illness and indeed there is proof that by helping sufferers through bio-psycho-social methods, our life can improve drastically. I now move on to the essays, which I have written over the years, that cover the above-mentioned areas of concern. In the conclusion, I will attempt to give an accurate definition of what mental disorders are to me and the many essays included in the book will help to support my answer.

8   Liberalism and its Human Nature

There is a specific and problematic human nature that has emerged in capitalist society. There is no doubt in my mind that this human nature contributes to mental illness, especially when people cannot live up to it, and I will here explore some aspects of human nature to make my point clear. It's not that there has been an ideal social system in the past or in the present. However, I will argue that a better social system is possible, particularly if we consider the Western and Eastern wisdom that have emerged through the centuries. The literature is full of suggestions and recommendation on how to achieve a better social order. It is greed and the patriarchal system which may prevent us from achieving a better world. It is our general and created social view that people with mental disorders are damaged and indeed many feel that there is no hope for them in that mental illness is often viewed as an illness like cancer but also a permanent malfunction that needs to be permanently treated with chemicals.

In this chapter I will discuss human nature, followed by myths and ideology. I will then consider the possibility of a better social system and for this, I have chosen the gift economy, proposed by a number of commentators, which already exists in our capitalist system, but in undeveloped form, that could bring about a better social system leading to much better mental health. I will then discuss creative anguish with a focus on the link between creativity and mental disorders, and then move to discuss childhood traumas, followed by a critical discussion of pharmacotherapy, therapy, and our current understanding of mental illness. Finally, I will attempt to suggest a possible direction for the near future if we are to reduce mental illness.

Liberalism emerged as a result of the Enlightenment and the revolutions of the 17th and 18th centuries. The Enlightenment was a movement of thought and beliefs concerned with reason, nature, and man. It was believed that through reason (i.e., that which was created within liberal democratic society) mankind could find knowledge and happiness (Hindess 1987:56).

The rise of scientific knowledge, philosophical thought, and the idea of general progress of all aspects of society gave people the belief that future happiness was in their hands. The creation of the idea that individuals could shape their future, including their fortunes or their failures, was to become one of the most devastating ideologies ever to emerge from liberal democratic policies. Such ideology emerged from a number of historical events that gave rise to a particular theory of human kind. While the industrial revolution created jobs, spurred innovation, science and medicine that made life easier and allowed social mobility, and money and time to pursue an education for some fortunate people, it also created tremendous problems for the disadvantaged, the disabled, and people of the third world countries. While the Industrial Revolution allowed some individuals the ability to look forward, many were stumped by its destructive forces.

There is reason to believe that the liberal theory of humankind originated within a dominant group of white Anglo-Saxon Protestants. This is because the Protestant religion, particularly in America, promoted private property, accumulation of wealth, and many features that are typical of liberal democratic policies (Weber 1958:46). In fact, it is written into the *Declaration of Independence*.

According to Weber, while India and China had technological knowledge, long before the Anglo-Saxons did, they lacked a religion that facilitated and encouraged the development of capitalism. According to Weber, "the ascetic Protestant had a quite different attitude to wealth and Weber believed that this attitude was characteristic of capitalism" (Haralambos 1995:46).

For Weber this attitude was a kind of religion that made possible a very solid system of practices and ideas that have today evolved into capitalism. Calvinistic Protestantism was just the right religion for the emergence of capitalism and also for the establishment of a superior and dominant group more powerful than the others (Weber 1958:49).

To promote the notion that Anglo-Saxon Protestant Americans and British people were superior, there emerged the theory of the "survival of the fittest". This phrase was coined by the Victorian journalist of evolutionary science Herbert Spencer. He wrote:

> Fostering the good for nothing at the expense of the good is
> an extreme cruelty. It is a deliberate storing up of miseries for
> the future generations. There is no greater curse to posterity

than that of bequeathing them an increasing population of imbeciles and idlers and criminals. To aid the bad in multiplying, is in effect, the same as maliciously providing for our descendants a multitude of enemies (Spencer 1882:204).

Spencer maintained that the natural flow of the evolution of humankind would be seriously hindered if the "unfit", the poor, the weak, downtrodden, stupid, and lazy, were not allowed to die off. Spencer felt that this "truth" justified a society where the smart would survive by taking from the weak, using any measure available to them, and without government interventions. Spencer therefore opposed tariffs, poor laws, state banking, public education, and all forms of government regulation of industry (Spencer 1969/1884:144). What does this say about us people with mental disorders? Get rid of them? Let them die off?

Spencer believed that evolution began in a simple form and developed into complexity (homogeneity growing into heterogeneity) (Ruse 1986: 19). Ruse writes that for Spencer:

> Life's history took a path up from the most simple of organisms, to the most heterogeneous organism of them all: Homo sapiens (Ruse 1986:78).

We arrive at a distinct premise by coupling the concept found in the above passage with Spencer's belief that the "most fit" human beings would suffer if the less fortunate were to be helped. For Spencer, it is possible to get morality out of evolution since, according to his views, it is immoral to interfere with evolution. The ideas of Spencer were to become part and parcel of a particular kind of liberalism known as classical liberalism, based on the notion of the improbability of the human condition, according to which, man is in control of nature, and that if she/he chooses to do so, she/he can ameliorate her/his life. Such a view is still widespread today.

The theory of "the survival of the fittest" was to gain momentum when a version of Darwin's (1859/1968) theory of natural selection was wrongly used to substantiate Spencer's original position. What Darwin had said, basically, was that humans had evolved from a more primitive species (i.e., no original creation). Moreover, he proposed that species that adapted best to their environment would eventually lead to a separate species (Dawkins 1989:57). Darwin believed that evolution should be left alone and that humans should not interfere with it by changing its course. This was what had given momentum to Spencer's original proposition that no intervention should be implemented to provide for the less fortunate, but that they should be left to die. This was a great misunderstanding of

Darwin's theory because he was speaking of evolution not of dis-advantaged people.

It is clear that Spencer's beliefs were based on incorrect assumptions and that, therefore, Spencer had created a myth. This myth has had a substantial impact on the way people conceive human nature today. Classical liberalism, in its developed contemporary form, still operates today in the corporate world. We can find proof of this contained in the writings of many contemporary commentators.

For Ruse, it is not possible to go from the language of morals (ought language) to the language of fact (is language). The two are logically distinct. I tend to agree with Ruse because "is language" is no more nor less than what humans understand at a particular historical time. This understanding is not fixed but changes as scientific discoveries are made and as new understandings of life are gained. Therefore, the "is language" is temporary. If the "is language" is not fixed, it follows that the "ought language" will also change at particular historical times. What ought to be the case today may not be the case in the future. Another problem with Spencer's attempt to link "is" with "ought" language is that one is supposed to get morality from evolution itself, not from man, who is one species out of thousands of species living on Earth. Moreover, there is no evidence that the fittest will always survive.

Of course, the fallacy of Spencer's theory is that all these characteristics depend on genetics alone. In fact, environment and heredity interact in very complex ways. For example, IQ is only mildly influenced by heredity, and then through very complex environmental mechanisms. Modern teaching methods can help even Down Syndrome sufferers to achieve a near-normal level of performance. In fact, the problem of today's world is whether to invest in the provision of special techniques to aid disabled persons so that they can function relatively normally in society. We have the wealth and technology to do so, but it remains a problem of redis-tribution of wealth. Put another way, it is up to wealthy multinational corporations and governments, ultimately, to decide whether or not to invest in disabled people. In my personal research and from my perspective, I have found many disabled people to operate at above normal levels of social intelligence and I have proof of this, which I will provide in the following chapter, where I present the personal experiences and perspectives of many disabled people who speak about human nature as they perceive and experience it.

Marx had made it quite clear that man was a product of the particular mode of production of his society. I feel that this is partly correct but not the whole story. This implies that, because the human animal is an active participant in the development of his/her mode of production, humans can overcome all of their problems, changing to an "ideal" mode of production. This is very simplistic. There are forces that are beyond the capacity of an individual at work in the shaping of a culture. Nevertheless, it is worth looking at Marx's theory because it reveals something of the utmost importance and that is that cooperation and love are just as strong as selfishness and greed.

To understand how human nature is not fixed but adaptable and flexible, Aristotle, followed by Marx, had come up with a theory that human nature is driven by drives and capacities and how these are satisfied or repressed has a great bearing on the kind of human nature that emerges.

According to Aristotle and Marx, drives are human manifestations such as feelings of hunger or thirst that drive the individual to seek gratification by either eating or drinking. In this sense, as Leahy argues (1975:3), drives are not unique to humans alone but also to animals. Animals too feel hungry and thirsty and as such have a natural tendency to satisfy these needs. So Marx and Aristotle believe that humans, unlike animals, have capacities such as rational thought, compassion, or creativity in art, science, or similar. Marx argues that in capitalist societies and particularly first world countries, animal nature is almost always satisfied (that is, that the majority of the population will be able to eat when they are hungry) but capacities are often repressed. Humans may not always be able to satisfy their capacities to be compassionate, to give gifts, or to be creative in their society, because capitalism is a mode of production that often prevents the fulfillment of such capacities. Some elitist members of the capitalist system may be able to fulfill all of their drives but for the majority of the world's population, it is more likely that these drives will be unfulfilled. Marx sees human nature as based more on the social animal than on the economic animal. As such, Marx recognizes that in a non-alienated society, based on a more sustainable mode of production, people's human nature would be different:

> In your satisfaction and your use of my product, I would have had the direct and conscious satisfaction that my work satisfied a human need, that it objectified human nature, and that it created an object appropriate to the need of another human being...I would have been affirmed in your thoughts as well as your love...In my production, I would have objectified my individuality and its particularity; and in the course of the activity, I would have enjoyed an individual life; in viewing the object, I would have experienced the individual life; in viewing the object, I would have experienced the individual joy of

knowing my personality as an objective, sensuously perceptible,
and indubitable power (Marx in Easton and Guddat 1967:281).

According to Marx, there seems to be an enjoyment that is felt by an
individual when he/she creates something or provides some service to help
another human. This enjoyment of social pleasure through production is,
according to Marx, an important part of the human capacities that are
repressed in capitalist society. This repressed state is part of what Marx
calls alienation and it comes about because of alienated labor. In this
respect, such alienation is due to a particular human nature that has
developed in capitalist society. What is important to establish now is that
for Marx, at the heart of a sustainable mode of production, there is a
human nature that is not alienated.

Alienation is a complex concept, one that was debated back at the
times of Greek philosophers like Plato (Mandel 1973:25). There are many
views on alienation. Some theorists claim that alienation is an integral part
of human life and in the Existential tradition rejects the notion that
alienation can be eradicated (ibid). Some Socialists claim that alienation is
a dominant feature of capitalism and that when capitalism is eliminated,
alienation will end (ibid). Perhaps alienation cannot be totally eliminated
in all of its manifestations. There are, nevertheless, some aspects of alienation that could be eradicated. For example, Marx proposed that there are
two important theories of alienation, namely alienated labor and the
alienation of humans from their capacities.

In Marx's terms, alienation is the "…estrangement either of man from
nature or of man from the means of productions via the labor process"
(Johnson 1981:8). Marx reasoned that the increasing population and
production along with power and commerce are: "…the necessary pre-
conditions of the division of labor" (Fisher 1970:39). For Marx, the
division of labor signaled a new human nature of mental and physical
crippling.

Looking at the difference between the mode of production of feudalism
and that of capitalism, Marx reasoned that in feudal society, craftsman
were "still at home with themselves producing something round and
complete for all of its limitations" (Fisher 1970:39). The craftsmen of
medieval times were totally dedicated to their work and were able to begin
and finish a given job. For example, cabinet makers would cut their work
and were able to cut their wood from logs and make their own glue. They
would complete every step of the work themselves and arrive at the
finished product much like artists are able to complete their work of art
from beginning to end (Fisher 1970:39).

In contrast, most workers today are alienated from the product they make in the sense that they seldom, if ever, complete a product. They assemble pieces that come already made from other industries and, in most cases, operate machines which become "...independent of the workman, who becomes its mere appendage" (Marx 1952:207). This, according to Marx, becomes a sort of torture since the machine "...does not free the laborer from work but deprives the work of all interest" (Marx 1952:208). According to Marx, workers sell their labor to the capitalist in order to live. Labor itself becomes a commodity. To explain alienated labor, Marx writes that in feudal times, the serfs did not sell their labor power but donated a tribute in the form of fruits of the land to their Lord (Marx 1847/1978:205). The workers in capitalist society, on the contrary, are forced to work and exchange their labor for money. For example, Marx writes:

> And the worker who for twelve hours weaves, spins, drills turns, builds, shovels, breaks stones... etc., does he consider this twelve hours as a manifestation of his life? On the contrary, life begins for him where this activity ceases, at table, in the public house, into bed...the twelve hours labor has no meaning for him (1847/1978:205).

This sort of argument led Marx to conclude that in capitalist society, humanity had become dominated by economics. Inevitably, this was seen by Marx as a moment in the history of humanity where individuals had lost the understanding that "...material life is the basis not the purpose, of human existence" (Fisher 1970:44). The purpose of human existence was to: "realize in labor the creative activity carried out in cooperation with others by which people transform the world outside themselves" (McLellan 1973:163).

Marx believed that "objects appropriated by man, acquire the power of owning man" (Fisher 1070:40). Marx identified four manifestations of alienation: (a) alienation which occurs when the workers are alienated from the product of their labor since what they produce is appropriated by other people. Thus they have no control over the fate of their product (McLellan 1987:149); (b) the workers become alienated from the act of production. Work becomes a commodity which is sold, its only value being its salability. This is because, as was previously stated, the workers are alienated from the product of their labor; (c) the workers become alienated from their human nature because alienation deprives them of those activities which distinguish humans from animals; (d) finally, the workers are alienated from other people since capitalism transforms social relations into market relations (ibid). This last concept of people alienated from people and from themselves is a discussion that I will explore in the next chapter where I present some alternative communities and I quote some people who have been living in a non-alienated environment for some decades now. For now, what is important to understand is that for Marx, when producers offer their product as a gift to another person, or when this product has a special meaning that bonds people together and therefore leads to fulfillment of drives and capacities, within the context of small communities, they satisfy their own needs.

Marx's theory of human nature was somewhat more complex than that of liberal discourse, which is very limited. However, liberalism was not one creed so it would be best to think of "liberalisms"—i.e., in the plural. I now turn to the welfare liberalism.

A different kind of liberalism emerged from the ideas of Adam Smith (1886) and those of Stuart Mill. This liberalism was to become known as "welfare liberalism". The welfare state based on this philosophy has operated particularly in countries such as Sweden, which provides the best historical example of the welfare state; however, it is today being undermined by a kind of ideology similar to that of Spencer although not quite as severe in that many disadvantaged and disabled people are provided with some basic provisions in terms of welfare payments, but the wealth is concentrated in the possession of a small proportion of the world's population and the gap between the "haves" and "have nots" is widening.

Stuart Mill (1859/1996:110) had a different idea about humans from that of Spencer. He believed that by providing an environment suitable for the stimulation and therefore rise of the moral and mental capacities of "all" people, society as a whole could be improved. This distinct view is what separates Mill from other liberals of his time. Moreover, both Smith (1776) and Mill (1996/1859) realized that the market could not provide for all the members of society and that interventions would be needed to bring a better distribution of wealth and resources.

Adam Smith observed that it was neither rationally nor morally sustainable to expect individuals to provide for all their needs and for all contingencies. He went on to argue that the state ought to provide for educational and health needs of the population and that this too was good for society in general (1859/1996:112). The ideas of Spencer and Mill were to have a great influence on the way people conceived of human nature and many writers have written along their lines of thought.

If both Smith and Mill were alive today, they would probably conclude that there are serious problem with the present corporate world. They would in all probability observe that poverty, world famine, and environmental degradation are all increasing, and this signals that the corporate world is in serious trouble and that the very existence of humanity is in danger. Future generations are destined to deal with apocalyptic visions of the future and the fear of losing their world. This is because of ignorance, greed and selfishness that derive directly from the human nature that has been created in the corporate world. Indeed, today the problem of redistribution of wealth is a first priority in economic debates about the economic future of our world.

On one hand, we have multinational corporations that are piling up the wealth and investing it so that it serves their interest (to increase their wealth in an obscene manner), while resources become more and more scarce and expensive for the majority of the world's population. At one stage, these multinational companies, in order to continue to make profits, will need to let go and give back some of their wealth, but the ideology of greed and selfishness prevents this. The only thing that could bring salvation, it would seem, is to nurture a compassionate and loving human nature based on the notion of the social animal not the survival of the fittest.

Firstly, there is no evidence that animals and particularly humans are selfish. To the contrary, Dawkins, in his book *The Selfish Gene* (1989), argues that the genes, in their instinctive struggle for survival, and indeed to increase their numbers, do act both selfishly and altruistically. Such phenomena can be seen at work in the animal and plant world and Dawkins provides many examples throughout his book

Kropotkin's theory of mutual aid contained in his essay titled *Mutual Aid: A Factor of Evolution* (1902) proposes that human nature is not "naturally" competitive and selfish. Selfish and competitive aspects of human nature have been nurtured and promoted by distorted accounts of Darwinian Theory that, according to Kropotkin, was misinterpreted. Using his observation of animal behavior, he concludes that there is no evidence for the claim that nature, animals, and humans have natural and dominant selfish tendencies. There may be single instances of selfishness, but mutual aid seems to be a much greater and more important force in nature for the preservation of a species.

Arguing in favor of cultural reforms for a better future, Singer writes that while humans have general tendencies to be violent, they are also very much co-operative and loving creatures. For Singer, there is just as much unselfishness as there is selfishness and he provides clear examples of this. For Singer (1993), the kind of human nature that has been created within liberal democratic society, which is essentially selfish, could lead to the extinction of humanity through self-destruction.

Singer presents some evidence to support his position that while both violence and love are human characteristics, love, co-operation, and altruism are strong human tendencies. To explain this, Singer brings forth the example of the family and how parents look after their children. He writes that:

> Biologists classify an action as altruistic or unselfish if it reduces one's "reproductive fitness"—that is, one's prospects of leaving descendants. Hence they often fail to acknowledge that what happens between parents and children is a step beyond egoism at all (1993:91).

Some strong evidence to support the notion that human nature is cooperative and social rather than selfish and alienated is found in the work of Israeli paleontologist Yoel Rak, who explains that for most of our evolutionary past, there were many humanoid species from which Homo sapiens could have developed. He writes:

> Think of that bar scene in *Star Wars*, where you see all kinds of aliens playing and drinking and talking together. I believe that image gives a better flavor of our evolutionary past (2000:16).

Since Darwin, it has been thought that biological supremacy was the key to human survival. But recent findings present a new theory. While selfish, unsocialized Neanderthal man died out because he had no friends, it seems that caring, sharing Homo sapiens survived because he discovered community values. The new theory supports the idea that the reason why Homo sapiens has survived all the other humanoid species, such as Neanderthal, is because of our social skills and our ability to work in cooperation but perhaps, most importantly for a reason that Dr. Bob Rich, who is a member of the Moora Moora cooperative, writes:

> Moora Moora is an intentional community. In 1974, a small group of idealists invested more money than they had, and bought a magnificent but sadly run-down property. Their aims were to care for the land, live cooperatively, and to be a source of education for society at large. They set up a pilot study in a saner lifestyle. My wife Jolanda and I first visited Moora Moora in 1975, joined in 1976, and moved onto the land in 1979. Our children grew up here, to their great benefit. Kids raised at Moora Moora are creative, self-reliant, independent, resourceful, and able to deal assertively with all ages.
>
> A cooperative lifestyle, in a place of grandeur and beauty, has good effects on adults too. However, there are negatives as well. You need to learn to say "no" without giving offense, and to accept it from others without taking offense. We are all raised in

an aggressive, competitive, egotistical society, and these attitudes are not left behind. Cooperation can be difficult. Human beings are genetically designed to live in small groups where group members are vitally significant to each other. Part of the alienation and unhappiness in society is because family units are too small, and other groupings too large. However, the downside is that within a community, it's harder to walk away from conflict (Rich, 1999).

Sociologist Peter Cock in an interview with Lisa Mitchell of *The Age* newspaper says:

> We're social beings and communicating on the email and phone isn't going to do it nor is investing in one other partner as the savior of our lives… But we're socializing people who can't cope with waiting five minutes. We're living in cuckoo-land and the ground stone of our times is very superficial and potentially, very explosive. (Mitchell, 2003. p12).

Elias Canetti in his work titled *Power and Crowds* (1962) argues that humans are not only independent self-sufficient beings with a unique mind. Humans are also very social beings with a crowd mentality. He writes:

> As soon as a man has surrendered himself to the crowd, he ceases to fear its touch. Ideally, all are equal there: no distinctions count, not even that of sex. That man pressed against him is the same as himself. He feels him as he feels himself. Suddenly, it is as though everything were happening in one and the same body… The crowd… suddenly they were there where there was nothing before… is a mysterious and universal phenomenon (*Canetti, 1962: 76, 84*).

Here we find Canetti's main argument that humans function not only at the individual level but essentially at a social one, specifically at the "crowd" level. Moreover, the crowd assumes a distinct nature from that of each of its individuals from which a very distinct crowd mentality and crowd behavior emerges at once independent from the mentality of each individual and yet a combination of the minds that form it. There is a crowd mentality here that needs to be studied if we are to understand human nature more adequately. And it follows that there must be human drives (both positive and negative) that can only be fulfilled in crowd participation and behavior.

Canetti's book sheds some light on this crowd mentality and crowd nature that seems to be a natural and common phenomenon also found in many animal societies. Canetti's underlying message is that we are social animals and that there is an urgent need to study humans in terms of how they function in social situations; we need to study closer, in Canetti's terms, the "crowd mentality".

The human nature that has been constructed in today's corporate world is very selfish and greedy and there seems to be hidden mechanisms that have developed which serve to mask the great inequalities and social injustice. To give an example of how ideology works, I now include two short essays, one on the tension between clinical and counseling psychology, and the other on the ongoing debate of the science and art aspects of psychology.

Clinical and
Counseling Psychology

I here contrast clinical and counseling psychology from the perspective of a perceived tension between the biomedical model of health, which does not take into account individual and social aspects of health and wellbeing, and the biopsychosocial model where it is believed that mind, body, and culture interact together to affect a person's health and wellbeing. There is a movement toward the biopsychosocial model and evidence indicates that counseling psychology is better positioned to embrace and promote it; hence the importance of preserving counseling psychology as a distinct endorsed area of practice.

Counseling and clinical psychology are two endorsed areas of practice accredited by the Australian Psychology Accreditation Council (APAC). I submit that both need to be preserved because they are two sides of the same coin. A merger of the two could arguably leave an opening for the biomedical model of mental disorders, best defined as the *Pax Medica* by Linford and Arden, (2009, p.16), to gain greater influence on psychology.

Evidence suggests that in Australia pharmaceutical industries (which favor the biomedical model) have an undesirable influence in medical schools and particularly on medical students. The problem of conflict of interest has been the focus of media attention, journal articles, books, newspapers, and research (Mason, Martin, and Tattersall, 2011, p.121).

Counseling psychology has provided a good opposition and scrutiny to the biomedical model while, at the same time, has enriched the field of psychology as a whole. I argue that counseling psychology is best placed to oppose the negative aspects of the biomedical model, while clinical psychology is extremely vulnerable to it. I will compare their differences, taking into consideration a struggle between the biomedical and biopsychosocial models and conflict of interest in Australian universities.

The differences between clinical and counseling psychology are not immediately obvious and in recent years, such differences have become even less noticeable (Norcross et al., 1997; Norcross et al., 1998; Norcross, 2000). This has prompted some commentators to call for a merger of the two (Watkins, 1985; Watkins, Lopez, Campbell, & Himmell,1986) while others maintain that it is questionable whether both specialties share the same philosophy in terms of health care provisions and preventative interventions (Zook,1987).

The differences may be traced historically, where we find a split between: (a) Freud's study of the unconscious mind, which led to therapy, and the humanistic theories of Carl Rogers with his idea of the person-centered approach (Davidson and Neale, 1990, p.54); and, on the other hand, (b) the behaviorisms of Watson and Skinner, which has dominated clinical psychology in the 50s and is still a strong component of clinical psychology (Burton et. Al, 2012, pp.13,14).

What exactly are the differences?

Clinical psychology courses have more focus on psychopharmacology and more psychopathology (Olujie, C., clinical psychologist, personal communication 28, March, 2012; Corcoran, P., clinical psychologist, personal communication, 14 April, 2012; Rich, B., counseling psychologist, personal communication, 12 March, 2012). Counseling psychology has more focus on family dynamics, a wider spread of therapeutic techniques, not just CBT, and a bio- psycho-social approach (Dluzewska, T., personal communication, 12 March, 2012). Both require knowledge of statistics, research methods and biology and are pretty full on regarding research (ibid). Competencies of the Australian Psychological Society (APS, 1997) clearly show the above-mentioned differences of core subjects, in terms of curriculum content

Both counseling and clinical psychology require intense training of at least four years of undergraduate studies, followed by two years of postgraduate studies. In addition, both include a Ph.D. degree, although only a few Australian Universities offer the Ph.D. degree in counseling psychology: three Universities in Victoria and one in Western Australia (Grant, Mullings and Denham, 2008, p. 3). In contrast to this, all Australian Universities offer studies in clinical psychology (ibid).

Clinical psychology is more likely to deal with a greater number of patients with severe mental disorders and often work side-by-side with psychiatrists, particularly in mental health clinics (Olujie, personal communication, 28 March, 2012). Counseling psychologists deal with less severe mental disorders and a broader population, from couples experiencing marital problems to family therapy, group sessions, and to people with anxiety or depression. However, as Grant, Mullings and Denham argue (2008, p.4), unlike the UK or the US, there is an ideology that circulates in Australia whereby counseling psychology is mistakenly taken to be a school which deals with the more normal section of the population. This is not necessarily true, as many counseling psychologists treat schizophrenia and Bipolar 1 (ibid, pp, 4-5). They may not have as many cases of severe mental disorders as clinical psychologists, but they are also trained to offer therapy to such cases (ibid). While these differences may seem minor, there is also a substantial philosophical difference between the two specialties.

Looking at the philosophy of counseling psychology, we find that the aims are: "…(1) [to]…focus on the importance of helping relationships to positive client outcome; (2)…question the exclusiveness of the 'disease model' in mental health; and (3) [have]… emphasis on building strengths and well-being rather than focus exclusively on sickness" (Grant, Mullings and Denham, 2008, p.7). Does Clinical psychology follow the same philosophy?

Clinical psychology has embraced the biopsychosocial model but the biomedical model, with its emphasis on scientific research, and the tendency to focus on behaviorism, has still a strong hold in Australian universities (Roznic, 2006, p. 63). Grant, Mullings and Denham write that: "…Clinical psychology rejects the strict biomedical model but has struggled to adopt alternatives such as utilized by counseling psychology" (2008, p. 6). The concern, I argue, is that while counseling psychology has grown to strongly oppose the strict biomedical model of health, clinical psychology has its vulnerabilities to the biomedical model because of its close affiliation with psychiatry and to psychopharmacology and psychopathology, which have the tendency to focus heavily on scientific research, often leaving out of the equation individual and social differences. But what is so wrong with the biomedical model of mental health, may we ask? And does it really have a strong influence in Australian universities?

There were three major historical events which have given strength to the biomedical model and have led to the emergence of the Pax Medica:

> …(1) the identification of major disorders, such as Attention Deficit Disorder (ADD) and major depression; (2) Aaron Beck's idea that method is what matters in therapy, which led to supporting various categories of mental illness and which, in turn, led to the Diagnostic and Statistical Manual of Mental Disorders or the DSM-III (APA, 1980); and 3) the creation of the antidepressant Prozac, which boosted pharmaceutical industries to unprecedented high profits and related consequences (Linford and Arden, 2009, p.16).

These events contributed to a diversion from interest in humanism and the meaning of life to an interest in medication for treatment (ibid). Many people have been medicated ever since and the reality is that many people who could benefit from therapy, or a combination of therapy and medication, now rely on medication alone (Whitfield, 2009, p. 5). This has given tremendous power to pharmaceutical industries that are extremely wealthy today (Linford and Arden, 2009, p.16). It is important for me to stress here that medication is important in the treatment of many sufferers and that it can save lives. What I am against is the corruption and over-prescribing and therefore need to monitor the conflict of interest, particularly in Australian medical schools.

This state of affairs has been scrutinized closely by many commentators who write to expose the problems with corruption and conflict of interest, whereby the pharmaceutical industry has had a lasting influence on medical students, in medical schools, in universities, on GPs and medical specialists, and in most areas of health (Roznic, 2006; Whitaker, 2005; Whitfield, 2010). In America, so serious was the problem of corruption and conflict of interest that the American Medical School Association (AMSA) decided to investigate it with research that found evidence of corruption:

> ...Much of this attention is due to evidence that industry relationships can influence the attitudes and behaviors of medical students, with effects persisting beyond graduation." (Mason, Martin and Tattersall, 2011, p.121).

Given this information, one could be forgiven for speculating that there could be a hidden move, driven by influential pharmaceutical industries, to combine counseling and clinical psychology. While such move could also be a positive one, it is unlikely to have a positive outcome if indeed universities are affected by the influential powers of pharmaceutical industries. It is clear that a regulatory body, to monitor conflict of interest within Australian universities, is of mandatory importance, and yet missing in Australia (ibid, p.121). I submit that until we have a strong body to monitor conflict of interest in Australian universities, it is unwise to merge counseling and clinical psychology. There are indications that some changes are happening, which will affect psychology courses in universities (Grant, Mullings, and Denham, 2008, p. 10). Given the ideology that dominates in Australian culture, where clinical is considered to be better than counseling psychology, it would seem wise for psychology as a whole to preserve counseling psychology, particularly in consideration of the fact that there is still great tension in psychology between those who call for more art in therapy and far less science and from those who call for more science, seeing anything that is non-scientific as useless.

Psychology is both an art and a science: as a discipline, it belongs to the science realm; while its various specialties are applied and belong to the art world. However, how the science and art parts of psychology are defined, and which parts are more important, is at the heart of an ongoing crisis that has affected psychology since the 1950s. Science and art are connected in that they both begin with a creative idea, but they also complement each other. However, while science is an academic, rational pursuit, counseling psychology, which relies on the art realm of psychology, can be a non-rational pursuit, as I will discuss. I argue that, in agreement with Gardner, psychology needs a lot more art, given that its most important application is the study of the human mind.

My worldview is partly shaped by my direct experience of Bipolar II Disorder, as a sufferer. In this position, I know that psychology, especially the art realm, which I feel is much neglected in academia, has a lot to offer, not only sufferers with mental disorders but all people. I am concerned at the current direction that Australian universities have taken, influenced by powerful pharmaceutical corporations, which promote the scientific method, giving the impression that humans are biological machines that can only be helped with various drugs.

Let's imagine a spectrum of disciplines that begins on the far left with physics, which is the most scientific of disciplines that relies heavily on laboratory observation, testing, and equations; the next are chemistry, biology, sociobiology, anthropology, and sociology. As we move from the far right to the left, the disciplines become less scientific and more artistic as the subject matter becomes more historical, meaning that the subject has experienced historical events that are impossible to test in a laboratory setting.

To illustrate this, we could use the example of a snowflake: at the level of its atomic and molecular structure, it is non-historical, or at least much less historical, in that we can study its molecular structure; at the level of its life journey, from its formation on, it is historical in that, as it falls down to Earth, it is carried by currents and temperature changes which contribute to its intricate shape. For example, Griffeath (2010) has been able to create a computer model of how branching tips of a snowflake form in a laboratory setting, for which he has used billions of equations. But, as he claims, if we take away the controlled laboratory setting, it becomes impossible to mathematize a snowflake's history, for there would be the need of trillions of calculations.

Humans can be compared to snowflakes, in the sense that our brain-body physiology may be partly studied in laboratory settings; but it is impossible to study mathematically the experiences which shape our lives.

To make matters even more complicated, we humans live in a very complex world, where the mind leads the body-brain.

Regardless of whether the mind exists separately from the body/brain, or rises from the body brain, it does have an impact on material life. An example of this is the fact that in the 50s and 60s, women stopped breastfeeding their babies and used formula instead of their natural milk, in order to follow an ideology that told them that their babies would grow healthier if they drank formula. This was later proven to be wrong and shows how the mind, ideas, and beliefs have a material impact on people's lives.

To add to these complexities, there is the fact that humans, as Gardner (1995) suggests, are "storied" beings in that we make sense of our life in terms of the stories that we create in our minds and of which we are central characters. The strangest of all things is that here, we have the mind studying itself for our literature, and art is an attempt to understand the mind. Such stories and ideas lead to entire worldviews that, while like castles built in the air, have a tremendous impact on our mental and material life. Gardner sees the need for cooperation between creative writers and psychologists, for they both are interested in the study of personality, self, and will. Just like cognitive and neuropsychology have joined forces in academia, literature and psychology can join together to better understand the human psyche.

Faced with these tremendous difficulties, it is no wonder that psychology continues to be in crisis.

What is psychology? How I answer this question depends not only on what I read about the topic, but largely on my life experiences. My worldview is extremely important here, for psychology cannot yet be accurately defined, unless we use meaning. This is because part of the crisis is found in the debate about what psychology is and its direction for the near future. Only direct and specific examples can help us here.

As someone who suffers with a mental disorder (Bipolar II), and someone who has helped other sufferers online for some years now, I tend to agree with Gardner that the most important aspect of psychology is the study of the human mind/psyche, or the "trio centered person". However, I am not in agreement with his proposition that once the various sciences will have cannibalized psychology, the true psychology will be left. Practicing psychologist Dr. Bob Rich writes:

> Why not neuropsychology? There are legitimate questions there. All divisions are artificial, for convenience. One of the professors of psychology at Monash, when I was there, had his PhD in aeronautical engineering. Perfectly legitimate fusion of

different fields. Why not brain science and psychology? Or anthropology and psychology? Any phenomenon is a legitimate field of study, and the tools of science can be turned on to it. There is no need to justify basic scientific investigation in terms of potential usefulness (private email exchange, November 2012).

Do I agree with Bob Rich? Yes, I agree; but because neuropsychology and science have now taken a large chunk of psychology, too much, we are lacking in humanitarian studies. I feel that a healthy balance is clearly missing. I repeat that theories are not facts and we need to be careful. I will debate this point in the following essay.

10 The Science and Art of Psychology

Both science and art are important, as Jeremy Holmes writes in his book, *Between Art and Science* (1993). My worldview, mostly created from personal experience, tells me that the study of the mind is the most important thing for psychology. When you suffer with debilitating depression and feelings of mild mania, as I do, and you have learned to control these using your mind/spirit, to say that the mind is part of the imagination is irrelevant. Thanks to my mind, spirit, and my will, I can control moods. What I say to "psychology is a science" psychologists is that they are not going to convince me that the mind is useless and that we need to eradicate any artistic notion of it from psychological literature.

Dr. Colin Wilks writes: "psychology is a science"; psychologists such as Skinner have said "psychology is an art"; psychologists such as Gardner, would agree that the mind and the self arise from the combination of body and brain. However, Wilks also writes:

> ...while 'psychology is a science' psychologists see the fictional nature of 'the self' as grounds for banishing all talk of it from the realm of neuron-centered, scientific psychology, 'psychology is an art' psychologists see the fictional nature of 'the self' as the 'firm' foundation from which 'person centered-trio psychology[3]' proceeds. (2012, lecture notes).

To understand what Wilks says, we can begin with the behaviorists of the 1950s, like John Watson, who proposed that psychology was a hard science. He needed to eliminate any notion of the mind or self. Humans were biological machines, deprived of any humanness, whose behavior was a response to stimulus. Accordingly, he believed that laboratory experiments on animals would tell much about what it is to be human.

---

[3] The person-centered trio is defined as personality, self, and will.

The "randomized controlled path" of science could reveal how humans function. Unfortunately, animal experiments are limited in what they can reveal about humans. For example, while Harlow's earlier animal experiments on attachment were extremely helpful to expose the mental damage inflicted on orphanages' children, his later experiments on animal depression shed no significant light on humans. This is because humans have worldviews, unlike animals, which have a tremendous impact on their physical and mental health. In fact, the World Health Organization (WHO) describes health as: "a state of complete physical, mental and social well-being and not merely the absence of disease or infirmity."

Skinner rescued behaviorism from the serious blunder that many had exposed: "…evidently it ignored and even denied the inner aspects of our mental states…" (Churchland (1993, p25) and it "…attempted to specify in detail the multi-tracked dispositions said to constitute any given mental state." (Ibid). Skinner stated that yes, the mind does exist, but it is only a product of electrical and chemical workings in the brain.

Therapy, be it cognitive therapy or narrative therapy, has proven extremely valuable in helping people with mental disorders and various other problems. Driven by the idea that psychology could be a pure science, without need for art, gave Eysenck the belief that therapy was useless, a belief that he was able to sell to the general population (Eysenck, 1952, p:323). This opened the door wide to pharmaceutical companies that began to mass medicate entire populations with serious consequences. Only recently, after so many decades, have we begun to understand the dangers of taking psychotropic medication, especially for children and teenagers.

Medication is not the answer for all people. However, what is really important here is that science itself has found that the brain is plastic and that it changes itself through experience, particularly through narrative and cognitive therapy (Doidge, 2007). In many cases, medication and therapy work well together to help sufferers with mental disorders. Here we have proof that science and art can work together, medication being representative of the scientific progress and narrative or cognitive therapy being representative of art, where the therapist uses his/her intuition and creativity to step into the client's shoes, to understand his/her problems. Counseling psychologists often need to use irrational beliefs and ideas of the client in order to help them.

To conclude, what I have said so far, given that I favor the idea that psychology is mainly an art supported by science, I include an answer of psychologist Dr. Bob Rich to my question to him about his use of science in his daily practice:

My scientific background is useful to me in my work in two ways:

1. I approach anything and everything as a scientist should: skeptical in the absence of evidence, but open to evidence. Every belief is merely a model open to disconfirmation.

This is how I assess a client's set of presenting problems. (I don't like the concept of diagnosis applied to psychological distress, and will only provide one if the client or a third party requires one.)

I don't believe or disbelieve anything a client (or other party) tells me, but look on it from the point of utility: is this useful or harmful for the client?

2. I take the matter of evidence-based therapy very seriously. This applies to specific actions I take (as with "diagnosis," I think "intervention" and "treatment" are value-laden in the wrong direction, and contrary to the evidence of what works in psychotherapy).

However, "evidence" to me does not mean limiting myself to the "randomized controlled trial" path. That's very useful in research, but real-life clients would typically be eliminated from the sample because of multiple problems ("comorbidities") and other complicating factors.

I select the techniques I choose and suggestions I make completely intuitively, based on my empathetic response to this client at this time—because that's what the evidence indicates as being effective. (Personal email exchange, 2012).

[I fully agree with Bob Rich here.]

The crisis in psychology is due to the inability of academics to agree that, while the mind and the self may rise from the brain, the mind does have an impact on our material life. The laboratory scientific method is a useful and entertaining game but limited, and certainly not an end in itself. The real science that Popper defines begins with an idea to be proven valuable or not, an idea that in time will become obsolete. In this sense, we find that science and art share much in common in that they begin with an idea. Psychology is both an art and a science, but we have not yet begun to accurately define psychology, its science and art components and there are many questions that remain unanswered such as: Is Cognitive Behavioral Therapy really as useful as research claims? This particular kind of therapy is appealing to psychologists because it is based on research and evidence-based practices. However, it does not work as well as many commentators and academics would have us believe. In fact, there are myths around CBT that need to be uncovered. In the following essay, I look closely, although briefly, at these problems.

Cognitive Behavioral Therapy (CBT)

Cognitive Behavioral Therapy (CBT) is a therapy much respected by academic psychologists. It is a method that can be tested and is based on the scientific practitioner model. In other words, for us students of a university, best to praise it than to criticize it. In fact, I would not waste much time criticizing it. Looking at its qualities and the research that supports it may be the better option for now.

I wish I could be more specific when I say that CBT does not work for me. I am just trying to give you an understanding of my experiences as someone who suffers with mood disorders. All I can say for now, because to enter into a discussion would be very complex, given that I would have to enter uncharted territory, is that I, like many other sufferers, do not just think cognitively but also emotionally and physically. My thoughts are a combination of emotions, behavior, and cognition, and sometimes emotions lead the way, getting to the thought first before cognition and behavior.

In order to cope and control my distorted thinking, I have to detach myself form our cultural practices and look at society and our way of thinking very critically. This has taken me to see the irrationality of our world. We are all irrational, for we do things that have a self-contained logic that often makes little sense. I question everything now, including myself. I try to look at myself critically and in particularly I try to look at the situation I am in. In other words, I question everything that comes to my mind, not just some things. This is a time consuming effort that makes life quite complex. But it is the only way that I can make sense of my life so that I need to do it.

To give you an example of why CBT does not help people who suffer with severe mental disorders, I include here parts of emails that I have received from friends. For example, here is the email of a friend, a mental health professional, who suffers with Bipolar Disorder:

"Our whole lives, we have been raised without any attention to distorted thinking or perception. How then are we ever going to see what is true, identify thoughts which have been used many times and accepted as true, with only minimal effort and 1 appt/week? For CBT to work, one must immerse oneself in it daily. Now does that sound easy? For myself, it does not work or does not really work well. I can stop and identify thought distortions but they are automatic and sometimes running in the background unnoticed.

I know what thoughts, what chain of distorted "reasoning" results in me feeling a certain way, having a certain perspective, and perceiving the world around me past and present. I see that they are distorted and can identify some of the sources of the distortion. Knowing all this does not change easily what I have engaged in for many years.

Rest easy, there are very few in this world that see with clarity, many of whom have spent a lifetime in this pursuit."

This other email is form a psychiatrist, who also suffers with major depression:

"Alfredo, I really do not believe that CBT would help me because the problems are much deeper than just learned, thoughtless behavior. Trauma changes everything and I some-times feel like the effects are in my bones. However, that has improved a lot with therapy. Working with EMDR has given me a lot of hope and I couldn't have gotten as far as I have without the help of my therapist, who is very skilled in this treatment method. I think CBT would be fine if you're just dealing with simple, incorrect ways of thinking and there's no underlying trauma. Just my opinion, of course, but one based on personal experience and learning from diverse literature on the subject."

And this is from a mental health nurse who suffers with a personality disorder:

"I think that CBT is in effect a bit of an insult to people like us who have good knowledge and insight into our own condition. CBT is very 'quick cure-all' and has been heralded as a great help to people who suffer from social phobia/depression/anxiety. To me, it is nothing short of pop psychology. Why?

Well, CBT is basically about changing the script, the message that we got as kids, that we are no good, hopeless etc., and we are to change our thinking; but it completely fails to address the human spirit. It fails to address the fact that many people who are labeled with Borderline, and indeed with Bipolar I and II, are in fact suffering from PTSD and there are, as you know, varying degrees of PTSD."

In many years of communication with sufferers, I am yet to find one person, out of nearly 1000, who tells me that CBT works for them. This remains a great puzzle to me, something that I have asked myself many times. If CBT is as good as they claim it is, and if there are so many statistics and research papers to back it up, why is it that I cannot find one person with a severe mental disorder who tells me that it works for them? I have asked a few professors and basically they tell me that even with research and statistics, we still see what we want to see. *What?* That has really shocked me because it means that scientific research may not be as scientific as we would like to think of it.

That is what I was told. Basically, sometimes we see what we want to see. To make this concept clearer, I include here an essay that I wrote on social phobia which explains a bit about Cognitive Behavioral Therapy (CBT) and related problems.

Social phobia is one of seven major anxiety disorders classified in the *Diagnostic and Statistical Manual of Mental Disorders* (*DSM-IV-TR*; American Psychiatric Association [APA], 2000) as the fear of social situations. The person having social phobia believes that he/she is exposed to the criticism and scrutiny of strangers. Three symptoms, described in the *DSM-IV-TR*, that have endured most days for at least six months, need to be present for a diagnosis of social phobia. Its prevalence rate is estimated at between 10 and 16 per cent of the population (Andrew, Creamer, Crino, Hunt, Lampe & Page, 2003) and statistics of co-morbidity with depression are quite high compared to other anxiety disorders (Douglass, 2001; Heimberg, Stein, Hiripi & Kessler, 2000).

According to Page et al. (2011), there are two main groups of social phobia: specific social phobia, such as fear of public speaking; and generalized social phobia where the person experiences anxiety in varied social situations. This discussion will describe symptoms of social phobia, which, according to Furmark (2000), can gravely affect a person's life and isolate them from society. It will describe the ways in which learning and cognitive theories explain how symptoms of social phobia occur and how cognitive and behavioral theorists have provided the foundations for the development of Cognitive Behavioral Therapy (CBT). It will then move to describe how CBT, which is a first choice evidence-based psychotherapy, supported by numerous research trials, works and how it is used to reduce symptoms. Finally, it will discuss limitations of CBT.

Behavioral and somatic symptoms vary in severity from extreme, such as panic attacks, to mild. General symptoms are: feelings of being restless, lack of concentration, feeling irritable, difficulties sleeping, and tension and fatigue (APA, 2000). Panic attacks comprise more intense symptoms. These arise from fear and related bodily functions that, while in some circumstances are quite normal (true alarms) and prepare the individual for danger (Cannon, 1915), such as when being chased by a dog or confronted by an armed criminal, are abnormal in social phobia (false alarms) (Page, Menzies, Bryant & Abbott, 2011). Release of adrenaline, or epinephrine, in the blood, triggers bodily responses to fear such as increased blood pressure and heart rate, dilated pupils, tension of the muscles, decreased digestion, closure or relaxation of the bowel and bladder, and increased sweating, which are known as the "freeze, flight, or fight" responses (Page et al., 2011). "Freeze" is the feeling of complete helplessness when all adaptive reaction stops; "flight" is the act of escaping to avoid danger, and "fight" is confronting unavoidable danger (Page, et al.). Females can have a different response to fear, known as "tend and befriend," a behavior that protects the self and others through nurturing (Taylor, Klein, Lewis, Gruenewald, Gurung & Updgegraph, 2000). Behavioral and somatic symptoms can arise from cognition.

According to Clark (1999), social phobia arises from distorted thoughts and beliefs about social situations, such as fear of other people's judgments and criticism, also known as "catastrophizing", a word that was first coined by American psychologist Albert Ellis. The main fear of this anxiety disorder is that the sufferer will exhibit their symptoms and behavior and consequently lose face in public (Clark, 2001). While the sufferers' obsessive desire is to find approval, acceptance, and respect from other people, because of past experiences, they will create certain assumptions about their social situations that will lead them to believe that they are in danger of being ridiculed, criticized, and disliked in such a way that severe and debilitating symptoms will arise, which will further fuel the anxiety (Clark & Wells, 1995; Freeman, Pretzer, Fleming & Simon, 1991). In particular, sufferers are terrified at the thought that people will notice their symptoms. Because of this, they may try to hide their anxiety, which may make their behavior, mannerisms, communication, and body movements appear strange to others (Clark, 2001).

Another cognitive symptom, which leads to avoidant behavior, is to think of ways to avoid social situations that are perceived as dangerous, especially those based on past negative experiences. Avoidance of social situations leads to missed opportunities with related costs (Page, et al.,

2011). These intrusive thoughts are cognitive symptoms that give rise to anxiety, which in turn leads to more intrusive thoughts. Clark and Wells (1995) name the cognitive processes of social phobia "the anxiety program", a negative cognitive program that can persist for years, unless the sufferer receives suitable treatment. Today social phobia is seen as a biological, psychosocial, and environmental problem (Barlow, 2002). Knowledge of and identification of symptoms is important in the description of social phobia and diagnosis, while Learning and Cognitive Theory are two major theories that shed some light on how social phobia develops.

Learning Theory attempts to study the etiology and perseverance of social phobia using classical conditioning, vicarious conditioning, and operant conditioning (Watt & DiFrancescantonio, 2010). For this theory, social phobia arises from learned experiences in the environment and the primary focus is on learning and behavior. Classical conditioning originated from the work of Pavlov, but is often associated with the 1920 Little Albert's experiments of J. Watson. This is a process of "paired association", where an individual is trained to respond to an uncon-ditional stimulus (Burton, Western, and Kowalski, 2012). In the case of social phobia, if an individual experiences heart palpitations and dizziness (arousal-related sensations) at the same time as the first unexpected panic attack, then the person may learn to fear heart palpitations and dizziness to the point that such sensations may trigger further panic attacks (Watt & DiFrancescantonio, 2010).

Operant conditioning, also known as instrumental learning, is mostly associated with the work of E. Thorndike and later B. F. Skinner. Skinner devised a method whereby negative or positive reinforcement and negative or positive punishment played the roles of strengthening (reinforcement) and weakening (punishment) certain behavior. For example, if a child was to complain of anxiety about going to school and the parents rewarded him by letting him skip school (positive reinforcement), this would tend to increase the anxious behavior (Burton et al., 2012). Vicarious conditioning refers to learning by watching and imitating other people's behavior, a theory that is supported by research (Page, et al., 2011).

For Bandura, cognitive processes are very important for the learning process and his theories provided a bridge between learning and cognitive theories (Burton, et al., 2012). For example, while a client may be aware of their irrational thoughts related to social phobia, they may be unable to help themselves because their neural pathways were created not only through cognition, but also through learning. Pavlov's idea that classical conditioning changes the activity of neurons that create the connection between action and response is supported by research (Bailey & Kandel,

1995). Because neural pathways and the brain can change, noted by Doidge (2010), people need to unlearn the unwanted behavior. Behavioral and cognitive modification programs are very useful in providing the right tools that clients can use to modify their behavior (Martin and Pear, 20XX). For Hofman (2008), cognition is critical to even the most basic forms of learning, and cognitive and learning theories work well together.

Cognitive theory has emerged out of the work of D. Meichenbaum, A. Ellis, and A.T. Beck (Corey, 2011). Beck's cognitive therapy had been inspired by Ellis' rational-emotive therapy. While the methods of these therapists differed in their application, they shared a main philosophy. At the heart of abnormal psychology, such as social phobia, there is dysfunctional thinking (Beck, 2011; Grieger & Boyd, 1980). For CT, the main problem is to be found in the way a client "perceives" a given situation, not the situation itself. It is based on a model that takes into consideration the relationship of cognition, behavior, and emotions (Freeman et al., 1990). CT focuses in particular on three aspects of cognition: "cognitive distortions", "automatic thoughts", and "underlying assumptions", which are also perpetuating factors. The A-B-C method, used by Ellis, best explains Cognitive theory's approach. "A" symbolizes the activating event, "B" the beliefs, and "C" the consequences or manifested behavior. From the CT perspective, it is not A (the event) that causes C (the consequences), but B. More precisely, it is the irrational beliefs that are at the heart of the problem (Corey, 2011). These beliefs can give rise to "automatic thoughts". Learning theory, RBT, and CT have led to the development of cognitive behavioral therapy.

Cognitive behavioral therapy (CBT), loosely defined, is a family of techniques that can be very powerful in inducing permanent change. It is based on the scientist-practitioner model where the therapist is constantly informed and guided by the scientific methods to ensure adequate operalization of the problems and measurement and testing of cognitive and behavioral changes toward the attainment of specific goals. In this sense, it is much more structured and goal-directed than other methods (Burton, 2012; Beck, 2011). CBT aims to teach sufferers how to control responses to stimuli that elicit fearful reactions that give rise to social phobia. By changing intrusive thoughts that generate anxiety, the unwanted behavior can be modified, therefore eliminating the anxiety's automatic responses. However, simply telling the clients to change their thoughts is not enough. Clients need to learn new skills, be dedicated to change and practice repeatedly the methods that will lead them to change their thinking (Neenen & Dryden, 2011). In addition, studies suggest that CBT works well for social phobia with co-morbidity (Stein and Stein, 2008). Both group and individual therapy are effective, with group therapy being considered the most effective because of its non-judgmental social interactions (Coles, Heart, Richard & Heimberg, 2001). Individual therapy is often preferred by clients because of the fear of strangers and of social situations. Two main techniques in particular are used to break the social phobic cycle: *exposure therapy* and *cognitive restructuring*.

The aim of exposure therapy is to desensitize the client to social situations which cause avoidance, fear, and anxiety in them. There are two kinds of exposure: in vivo or real-life physical exposure to the feared situation which, according to research, is the most effective treatment (Choy, Fyer & Lipsitz, 2007); and imaginable or mental exposure in preparation for the in vivo exposure (Page et al., 2011). Exposure to the most feared situation is known as flooding, but this method is used less often because most clients prefer to proceed gradually from the least fearful situation to the more feared ones (Pull, 2005). Cognitive restructuring is an effective method used to help clients identify their irrational thoughts, using a variety of strategies, including guided imaging, audio or video recordings of therapy sessions, and Socratic questioning (Page, et al., 2011).

By asking Socratic questions, the therapist creates therapeutic opportunities and helps the client develop strategies to cope with future problems by empowering them to become their own therapist (Carey and Mullan, 2004). Four procedures of cognitive restructuring, described by Hope, Burns, Hyes, Herbert & Warner (2010), can provide a framework for Socratic questioning, and these are: (1) the identification of automatic thoughts and related negative views of the self and the world; (2) identification of distorted thinking of the automatic thoughts; (3) philosophical and rational evaluation; and (4) restructuring of the irrational thoughts toward more positive outcomes. Socratic questioning aims to challenge the avoidance of social situations based on previous negative experiences (Beck, 2011). Another method of CBT is to give the client homework. Homework aids toward constant monitoring of improvement through measurement of attitudes and moods and it gives an indication of the client's commitment to the therapy, progress, or setbacks (Beck, 2011).

CBT is considered the most effective psychotherapy, especially if used in conjunction with pharmacotherapy (Heimberg, Liebowitz, Hope, Schneier, Holt, Klein, 1998). However, there are problems with medications which are not indicated for children and teenagers and which can have adverse side effects in long-term usage (Whitfield, 2011). CBT does not work for everyone (Cooper, 2008) and there are reasons to believe that when social phobia derives from the combination of genetic vulnerabilities and childhood traumas, it can be difficult to treat (Corey, 2011). One of the most recent etiology is that of Rapee and Heimberg

(1997), who propose that social phobics often begin their lives with overprotective and/or overly intrusive parents (Coles, Heart & Heimberg, 2001). For Cooper (2008), other therapies are equally effective and the idea that CBT is superior to other methods is a myth. Seeing CBT as a one-size-fits-all therapy is detrimental in that clients who could benefit from other methods miss out. Cooper also argues that the relationship between therapist and client is very important in determining outcomes, in line with the client-centered approach and ideas of Carl Rogers (1957). People with a fixed mindset do not benefit from any therapy, while those with a flexible mindset tend to make progress (Dweck, 2006). The environment is also important so that, for example, it is hard to expect people to "...think healthfully ...when working for an exploitative corporation?" (Tuggart, 2011, p 1). Humans are extremely complex beings.

What I find interesting is that Humberg proposes a new etiology of social phobia and anxiety, one more generally based on childhood experiences with overprotective and over-intrusive parents. Indeed, many mental disorders can be traced back to childhood problems, particularly problematic relationships between children and parents.

12 Childhood Traumatic Experiences

I have been doing research on childhood trauma for quite a few years now, although I haven't written anything concrete yet. Nevertheless, I have collected a lot of information and written extensively about some of the problems. From my perspective, a psychiatric disorder is nothing more than a kind of human suffering best described as mental anguish of either traumatic or creative origins.

This idea, which I call TAUTOA (Towards a Unified Theory of Anguish), is based on the findings of two sets of questionnaires, which have revealed that childhood trauma is the cause of many serious psychiatric disorders. This is supported by many psychologists and psychiatrists today as well as by current research findings (Read, 2006; Salmond, 2010; Whitfield 2010).

TAUTOA is not a scientific idea, but the mere voicing of an idea. It is not a quotable document any scientist would take seriously and yet its direction is important because, in my opinion, as I hope my personal research will show one day soon, it has far-reaching implications. These implications are:

a) If childhood trauma makes up the majority of psychiatric disorders, it is more plausible to think that the problems have an origin and a cause. If this is so, then it would make sense to move away from our tendency to look exclusively at chemical imbalances, as if they were the only cause of the problems, and focus on the causes which have triggered the problems in the first place.

b) If it can be argued that childhood trauma, and more generally all kinds of trauma, are at the heart of mental illness, then the biological explanation looses strength as an argument. Exposure therapy and hypnosis are sometimes very effective in the treatment of traumatic experiences by repeatedly exposing the sufferer to the traumas until adequate resilience is achieved.

c) When all of these complex issues are considered, it can be said that our direction, in terms of tackling the problem of mental illness, is wrong and leads to erroneous interventions and related waste of time and money. Therefore, the importance of this paper is to warn academics and mental health professionals that we need to take a different path, one based on healing and recovery interventions.

Dr Gabor Matè, who has published a number of books on the topic, argues that future susceptibility to a particular condition is a complex interaction of genetic weaknesses and strengths and learning by modeling the significant people in a child's life. Resilience is similarly determined. For a person to develop a serious adult "psychiatric disorder", it is necessary that subjectively perceived childhood abuse or neglect be experienced at any one time, and/or that a person experiences a certain level of environmental stress. If that sufficiently exceeds the person's resilience, a collapse occurs. The nature of the collapse, i.e., the symptoms and diagnosis, is a matter of the first point; and since the causation is the same, the details of the reaction are not that relevant. All this attention to diagnosis is misplaced. More important is building up resilience, and to allow the person to develop a new way of reacting to the world. A question pops up in my mind now: "If what we loosely call 'mental illness' springs directly from childhood traumas (or other kinds of traumatic experiences) is it plausible to think of psychiatric disorders as biological illnesses?"

Many argue that brain functions may be abnormal at the start before the traumatic experiences and that the trauma only exacerbates this condition. Even if this was so, it is hard to explain why childhood traumas are so central to the development of serious psychological disorders such as bipolar and schizophrenia.

TAUTOA questions the mainstream arguments placing emotions, experiences and consciousness as creators of psychological distress, which I like to call mental anguish.

According to TAUTOA, symptoms are responses to difficult life situations and as such are a cry for help. Psychological symptoms indicate underlying problems, which can either be medicated out of existence or used to get to the underlying cause. I am not saying that medication is not useful, but that it must be used with caution, unlike current practices where the trend seems to be over-prescription of drugs. These ideas are supported by some psychologists and psychiatrists (Omar Salem, 2007; Corry, M. & Tubridy, A., 2001; Linford and Arden, 2009; Wright 2006; Capra 1989).

TAUTOA makes it possible for us to understand mental disorders and move away from stigma and prejudice putting human suffering back into the healing process where it belongs.

Dr Bob Rich, who I consider my supervisor and collaborator in this project, has written the following explanation of the idea:

> Alfredo and I have been exchanging many emails about the nature of mental disorders, and more generally of suffering, whether it qualifies for a diagnosis or not.
>
> I have also occasionally communicated with Michael Gathercole, whose paper on depression is up on my website[4]. The work Alfredo and I are doing is logically an extension of Michael's, who has focused on one kind of suffering.

This is not the place for a theoretical analysis, the citing of endless items of evidence (which exist), or generating testable predictions. All that needs to be done and will be if we ever arrive at a scholarly paper. Here, we merely state our conclusions.

> 1. People vary in every way possible. All of us have genetic strengths and weaknesses. A weakness is only a potential, not a life sentence. For example, a genetic weakness to alcoholism will only be a problem for a person who abuses alcohol. Someone who drinks moderately, if at all, will never become an alcoholic. A person with a weak pancreas will probably avoid diabetes by keeping to a suitable diet.
>
> 2. Some genetic weaknesses predispose a person to a given kind of mental suffering such as anxiety, depression, schizophrenia, etc. Again, these are not preordained problems, but are risks that manifest in the right (well, wrong) circumstances.
>
> 3. Early childhood experiences either provide protection from genetic weaknesses, or trigger them. For example, a person who, early on, develops a self-view of being faulty could suffer either from depression or anxiety in adulthood. Which of these manifests will depend on the presence of the relevant genetic weakness.
>
> 4. Children who have inherited a tendency to develop a psychological problem are likely to be cared for by people with the same weakness. This can even be true for adopted children. Therefore, early childhood experiences are likely to combine with genetic weaknesses rather than to protect against them. For

---

[4] http://anxietyanddepression-help.com/gathercole.html

this reason, there is not much point in worrying about genetics. You can't change your kids' genes, but you can change how you bring them up.

5. A separate issue is *resilience*. This is the ability to stand up to stress, survive difficulties, thrive on challenges. It may also have a genetic basis. That is, some people may be naturally more robust than others.

6. However, resilience changes over the life span. It varies from time to time, situation to situation, and is affected by things like current physical health, the thoughts going through your mind and the company you keep.

7. At any one time, you are under a certain amount of stress. Its source doesn't matter that much. You can be stressed by work demands, life changes (even good ones), fatigue, illness, pain, conflict, grief, disappointment... all of these add up.

8. If the level of stress at this moment exceeds your resilience, then you will break. This break may be temporary or long-lasting, depending on many factors, including your thoughts about it.

9. Now we return to the beginning. When you break, the symptoms will be those determined by your genetic weaknesses and early childhood upbringing.

This means that the same causal processes will make me depressed, Alfredo bipolar, my friend Terry terrified (good pun?), and my friend Lisa schizophrenic. The symptoms don't matter. The label is counterproductive, and is not a guide to the required treatment.

Because the causes are the same, the treatment is the same. Outrageous as this statement may seem, it is actually supported by a huge amount of evidence. Studies of the factors influencing success in psychotherapy show that technique has a very minor bearing. Therapies with wildly different approaches have about the same success rate.

That doesn't make sense if we look at mental disorders as something like physical disorders, and psychotherapy as a medical-like cure. It makes perfect sense from our point of view.

Following these ideas, I wrote a journal article on childhood trauma and I include it below.

~ ~ ~

In this issue, I explore the topic of childhood trauma and its positive correlation with mental illness. While this is not a topic directly relevant to mental health stigma, it is important because there is much evidence to suggest that childhood trauma can trigger mental illness (Whitfield, 2010; Maté, 2000). In turn, mental illness fuels stigma. Therefore it is more than plausible to suggest that childhood trauma leads to mental illness, which in turn increases the level of stigma in society.

Today there is a tendency to label mental health disorders and to rely, perhaps more than we should, on psychotropic medication to cure these disorders. Many commentators argue that psychotropic medication is not indicated in cases where PTSD is the problem and every effort should be made to use talk therapy or other natural intervention before doctors rush to the pad to prescribe drugs (Whitfield, 2010; Corry and Tubridy, 2001; McKay and Zac, 2002).

According to some commentators, clinical diagnosis exacerbates stigma (Corrigan et al., 2000; Weiner et al., 1988; Anderson, 1991; Kashima, 2000). Although diagnostics are developed by mental health professionals, to better understand mental illness, the result is that diagnostic classification exacerbates the problem of stigma. Sociologists define *structural stigma* as institutional efforts that unintentionally lead to discrimination (Hill, 1988; Wislon, 1990).

There is also evidence, from statistics, to suggest that childhood abuse affects a great number of our children. A survey from my personal longitudinal research of nine years has revealed that about 75% of sufferers, out of a sample of over 700 sufferers, have endured traumatic experiences during their childhood. For example, many people who suffer with Borderline Personality Disorder (BPD) report having had a history of abuse and neglect. Many studies support these claims (Klaft, 1990; Zanarini, 1988; Brown and Anderson, 1991; Herman, 1992; Quadrio, 2005); and that childhood trauma is a risk factors for a diagnosis of schizophrenia later in life (Janssen, Krabbendam, Bak , et al, 2001). Some research indicates that childhood trauma is a causal factor for the development of psychosis and schizophrenia (Read, van OS, Morris and Ross, 2005).

I have also argued in previous issues of this journal that mental health stigma is increasing in western societies despite great efforts to reduce it. For these reasons, it makes good sense to suggest that perhaps our efforts in Australia should be directed toward reducing childhood trauma, a topic that is very often neglected by researchers and mental health professionals.

My longitudinal study indicates that what triggers most mental illness is childhood trauma. What has also become apparent from my research is that sufferers are almost always unaware of having experienced a childhood trauma until we start discussing past experiences. To give an example, this is what a sufferer wrote:

I don't think there is a cause for my depression and psychosis. I was sexually assaulted at 16 and my mother was an alcoholic, abusive and violent. But there does not seem to be any ongoing trauma from that.

This was by no means an isolated incident. The majority of sufferers either block the traumatic events from consciousness or, alternatively, they are genuinely not aware because they are so sure that it is a biological illness as in brain disease. When I read the email and saw that there was sexual abuse, as well as violence and alcohol involved, I became suspicious; so I asked a psychologist friend. This is what he wrote in an email:

> That kind of patter makes me strongly suspect repressed severe trauma. She should go to a good therapist and do age regression hypnosis. If there is trauma, and she recalls it, she can deal with it and get rid of the problem, sometimes for life. It usually feels too scary to do. I say to my clients: there is a box there, and you are working hard to keep the lid on. But what's in the box is not a monster. It's the photograph or movie of the monster. A photograph or movie cannot hurt you, only remind you of your past hurt.

One interesting fact that research tells us is that most homeless families are women and children escaping domestic violence, which is often sparked by excessive alcohol consumption and/or drug intake (Hansen, 2010). The Drug and Alcohol Services of South Australia (2010) reports that over 450,000 children, in South Australia alone, live in households where they are at risk of exposure to binge drinking by at least one adult. The Australian Bureau of Statistics (2004-2005) reports that one in eight adults (approximately 2.5 million people) drink at risky/high-risk levels.

As of this writing, in Australia, 12,133 children under the age of 12 are homeless. In addition, almost 28,000 young people below 18 years of age are homeless and their past has often been a traumatic one.

There are 7,483 homeless families and every day, 2 out of 3 children, who require immediate assistance, are turned away. These figures are quite alarming if we consider that Australia has a population of just over 20,000,000 people. (Homeless Australia)

In Australia, we have the Department of Community Services (DOCS), a department that monitors the welfare of the children. The problem is that for some reason, DOCS is failing to protect all, and perhaps most, of our children. In the *Sunday Telegraph*, Jane Hansen wrote that:

...a senior Community Services bureaucrat has claimed that caseworkers don't visit extreme cases of abuse and neglect for fear they will be blamed for the deaths of children. The official, who has made the sickening allegations, has also handed over files detailing serious shortcomings within the department. (Hansen, 2011)

From direct experience, as someone who has lived in a troubled government complex of houses, both my wife and I wrote numerous letters to ministers and government organizations before DOCS' caseworkers came to see children who had been abused or exposed to domestic violence, fuelled by alcohol and drugs. The caseworkers were unable to help the children, who continued to be exposed to violence and abuse for months after their visits.

The AIHW reported that in Australia, during 2009-10, there were 286,437 reports of suspected child abuse and neglect made to state and territory authorities (AIHW, 2010). We have to keep in mind that there are so many cases which are not reported for a variety of obvious reasons.

Traditionally, child protection data is considered to be a very conservative estimate of the occurrence of child maltreatment (Bromfield & Higgins, 2004). Child abuse and neglect often goes undetected because of the private nature of the crime, the difficulties children experience in disclosing and being believed, and lack of evidence for the crime (Irenyi, 2007).

Unfortunately, we are not able to get an accurate number of possible child abuse cases because, as a social worker commented during an interview with me, a more realistic figure may be that there are between 500,000 and 700,000 cases of child abuse each year. This social worker speculated that: "Thousands out there are terrified to pick up the phone. There have been hundreds of Social Workers who were 'afraid' to get involved because of threats of violence."

There are many statistics which show that Australian children are not well looked after by their parents or guardians. These statistics help in supporting the idea that mental illness and childhood trauma are strongly and positively correlated.

In recent years, many studies have attempted to demonstrate that symptoms of post traumatic stress disorder (PTSD) are not necessarily the result of traumatic experiences. Accordingly, commentators argue that these symptoms may have existed even in the absence of trauma. This kind of rhetoric is particularly helpful for those who consider mental illness to be a disease of the brain and therefore not always connected to environmental factors. One could say that pharmaceutical corporations would benefit from such ideas because if mental illness is considered to be disease, then medication is the only thing that will help. Fortunately, many studies disprove these false beliefs.

There is a particular study on twins which may quiet doubts over the debate on PTSD and traumatic events linkage. In this study of 103 pairs of identical twins, one twin had been exposed to combat in the Vietnam War, while the other had not. Pitman and colleagues from Harvard University and the US Department of Veteran Affairs found that men who had been at war had three-fold more symptoms than their brothers, as well as compared to the combat veterans without PTSD and their co-twins. This study tends to suggest that genetics or biology has little to do with PTSD and that there is a strong link between PTSD and experienced trauma. Research in the US (National Institute of Health, 2009) reveals that "a certain gene variation long thought to increase risk in conjunction with stressful life events actually may have no effect" (NIMH, 2009). To the contrary, there is strong evidence from research that stressful life events are strongly associated with a person's risk for major depression and psychosis.

There is plenty of evidence to support the idea that most mental illness is triggered by childhood traumas and perhaps this is the direction that research should follow.

Unfortunately, not much research is done on childhood trauma, perhaps because it is such a sad topic and one that does not lend itself to scientific enquiry. The researcher would have to come to the understanding that we, in our Western world, are damaging the minds of our children and that we are having a negative impact on their future in complex ways. Not many of us would like to admit this, for we like to think that the world is OK, that we have advanced technology, and that the future may be brighter and lead to improvements. In my opinion, we can no longer sustain such optimism, particularly in the face of the fact that our democratic system seems to be failing our children.

In this journal, I try to explore these complex issues with the help of sufferers who have endured childhood traumas directly. I hope that our voice contributes to the understanding that PTSD is caused by traumatic life experiences and not by innate and biological factors alone. For all of these reasons that I have discussed in this letter, it would make much sense to move away from the idea of mental illness as disease and begin to research childhood trauma and traumatic experiences more broadly.

I hope that this chapter prompts mental health professionals to pay more attention to childhood trauma and entertain the possibility that childhood trauma makes up the greatest percentage of mental disorder cases in our world today. It is clear that the important message here is that if childhood trauma indeed causes most mental illness, it would make sense to attempt to reduce childhood trauma because in so doing, we may well reduce mental disorders and related mental health stigma. While I have here presented the Australian situation around childhood trauma and neglect, the problem is similar in other countries. For example, the ACE study conducted in America has established a clear link between childhood trauma and the development of later ill health, including mental illness. For further information, see the website http://www.cdc.gov/ace/findings.htm.

In conclusion, I will say that there is a wealth of research which has revealed that children's life experiences, from birth till six years of age, have a powerful impact on the rest of their life. How does humanity treat their children? A quick look at the statistics of the world indicates that humanity does not treat their children well. Humanity traumatizes their children and it's making their future difficult, to say the least. Let's face it: we are stuffing our children's world with our greed, selfishness, and ignorance. We have evidence to suggest that what we call mental illness may largely be triggered by traumatic experiences, and because of this, much mental illness could be prevented. Yet humanity fails to recognize both the terrible treatment of their children and the fact that mental illness is the outcome of this treatment. For this reason, we use anti-psychotic drugs and anti-depressants much more than we should. This is our cognitive dissonance, the belief that we are not responsible for how and why our children develop a mental illness. Perhaps it is helpful to show here how I help sufferers because while I am not a therapist, I do use my creativity and my humanitarian gift to help others; and writing a bit about it may give an idea of our inner world—the world of a person who struggles with a mental disorder.

13 Internal and External Aspects of Multiple Personalities in Bipolar Disorder

The idea for this journal, which looks into the possibility that some sufferers experience internal conflicts that can be best conceptualized, metaphorically speaking, as different selves, came to me after having communicated with a sufferer—whom I will call Fatima—with Bipolar II.

In an email, she wrote that she was seeing a psychologist who was writing a paper on multiple selves in Bipolar II, and that she had contributed, as a client, to this paper simply by being a patient who had expressed this feeling of having multiple selves (metaphorically, of course).

Fatima recalls one of her conversations with her therapist, saying that she was like two people: the "Nice Fatima" and the "Monster Fatima". The Nice Fatima was organized, conscientious, calm, and in control; the Monster Fatima was really scary, moody, argumentative, rebellious, and someone who would verbally lash out at people or complain at the first opportunity. In other words, the Monster Fatima was a troublemaker that would cause problems wherever she went. But that was not her real self, Fatima stated. At other times, Fatima saw herself as euphoric, much like a child seeking attention; emotional, egotistic, disruptive, and grandiose.

Because I suffer with Bipolar II disorder, I can understand what Fatima is trying to say and I can relate to it, although I would not say that there is a Monster Alfredo to my personality. There is an argumentative and fussy Alfredo, however, that can have ideas of grandeur and become (hypo)manic. There is also the calm and in-control Alfredo, who can be very constructive, helpful and very caring. In fact, the good self of Alfredo is humanitarian and seeks truth. In this sense, I could relate to Fatima's description of multiple selves.

I decided to ask other sufferers of various disorders what they thought about the idea of different selves. What has been interesting so far is that most of us sufferers have experienced childhood trauma that has affected our personality and sense of self. While the idea of multiple selves may be more relevant to those like me, who suffer with Bipolar II (in my case, cyclothymia), it can be useful to those who suffer with depression and other disorders because it opens up a discussion where we can talk about shattered selves, aspects of one's personality that have become hidden because of a traumatic experience, and so on.

It is becoming clear that our personality has been affected in some way and that discussing the metaphorical idea of different selves may be helpful, even if it is not directly suitable to disorders like Dysthymia or Depression. For Bipolar II disorder, there seems to be some relevance because we do feel like different people at times, due to our changing behavior and alternate states (depression/[hypo]mania).

When I am (hypo)manic, I am a very different person from when I am depressed. This is like having two different selves. In the past two years, I have been able to really work on my moods, symptoms, and personality so that I am much more in control. I find that discussing the idea of different selves may open up dialogue that could help me even more in the future.

Becoming aware of the shattered selves, different selves or hidden aspects of one's personality could be therapeutic and empower us to better understand and manage our disorder. After all, there is an adult, a child, and a parent personality in all of us, just like Dr. Harris once wrote in his book, *I'm Ok, You're Ok*.

One thing that becomes immediately apparent is that the self and personality are not fixed but that they can change over time—if not fully, then partly. It is a fact to say that I have seen tremendous changes for the better in sufferers like myself, Rose, and Judy over the past three years. We are all becoming more humanitarian and more understanding of our disorder. Helping people and helping ourselves in the process is the key to better health.

According to what various sufferers have written to me in the past six years, the idea of multiple selves is not only appropriate for some, but it can also serve as an opening for a debate about personality aspects of our disorder. Nevertheless, I must value Dr. Bob Rich's idea that the language of different selves is confusing and that people with DID experience the real different selves in the real sense of the word, while we only experience it as a kind of metaphor (i.e., having multiple selves for some of us is more abstract than concrete).

Does the biochemical dysfunction of our brain cause the moods and symptoms, and therefore affect our personality? Or does the trauma that we experience, particularly as children, trigger the mental disorder and therefore affects biochemical functions of our brain? This is a chicken-or-egg question for which we have no clear answer. Many studies tend to indicate that childhood trauma is very frequent amongst sufferers.

For example, in case of personality disorders, research estimates that trauma may be as high as 98% as a trigger for the disorder. I feel that it could well be the same for bipolar, dysthymia, depression, and schizophrenia. We need to keep an open mind. If mental illness is triggered by trauma in children or people who are more sensitive than the rest, then we may well be looking at the whole concept of mental illness from the wrong perspective. Medication is important as part of the therapy and some people will need medication for life. But this is not a conclusive proof that our disorder is biochemical. The recovery movement, the plastic brain, and other complex understanding of how humans function may well point to a different road to take, the road less travelled.

Perhaps it is our ignorance and way of life that really causes what we call mental illness. Our voices call for more inclusion of psychological interventions and environmental modification that facilitate recovery. The self is not fixed and mental disorders are not necessarily a lifetime sentence. We may need to change our perspective on things, and working on our feeling of having multiple selves may just be the required opening. We also need to discuss problems with the tendency to medicate people and rely on pharmacotherapy alone where other methods are often required. I now include an essay on antipsychotic and antidepressant drugs.

14 | Antipsychotic and Antidepressant Drugs

There were three major events which gave rise to the Pax Medica era, and these were: (1) the creation of the antidepressant Prozac; (2) Robert Spitzer's identification and labeling of three major disorders, namely, panic disorder, attention deficit disorder (ADHD) and major depression; (3) Aaron Beck's model of psychotherapy based on the erroneous view that technique is what matters in therapy, therefore supporting various categories of mental illness, which in turn influenced the new version of the Diagnostic and Statistical manual of Mental Disorders or the DSM III (American Psychiatric Association, 1980). (Linford and Arden 2009, p: 17).

Beck's presentation of the new therapy model, and Eyseneck's critique of psychotherapy based on technique (Eysenck, 1952, p: 323), was probably what made therapy less effective and seen as second to medication treatment. There is no doubt that these three major events gave way to the pharmaceutical companies that began to make huge profits from the sale of psychotropic drugs. This was a global phenomenon which led to some well-documented incidence of corruption. Excessive marketing of pharmaceutical companies, the fact that many psychiatrists had bought into the industry at the expense of the patients, and the fact that medication is not always effective and that the side effects can be deadly or lead to severe illness were somehow masked by the ideology that became stronger from the 1970s onwards.

In the 1970s, psychotherapy became a second-rate alternative treatment with antidepressants and antipsychotic medication being the first choice. (Linford and Arden 2009, p:16) The advent of the medication Prozac can be considered a watershed in the history of mental illness. The drug came out in 1974 and "created a profound shift in psychiatry away from interests in meaning and toward a fascination with medication." (ibid) This phenomenon continues to this day where in the U.S. alone, more than 20 million prescriptions of Prozac are written annually and, by contrast, only one in twenty patients in America sees a psychiatrist or psychologist (Linford and Arden 2009, p: 17).

Prozac is Fluoxetine and belongs to the selective serotonin reuptake (SSRI) class. The work that led to the discovery of Fluoxetine was due to collaboration between Bryan Molloy and Robert Rathbun, who were working at the pharmaceutical company Eli Lilly back in the 1970s. Tests began and the drug continued to be refined until it was finally released as an antidepressant after having been approved by the Food and Drug Administration (FDA) in the U.S. in December of 1987. In 2001, Eli Lilly's patent expired, giving way to an influx of various generic brands. Prozac was re-branded Sarafem "in an attempt to stem the post-patent decrease in Eli Lilly's sales of Fluoxetine" (Selena, 2009, P:3).

Eli Lily's various marketing campaigns ensured that Fluoxetine became known as the most efficient and popular antidepressant on the market. The drug worked by increasing serotonin and nor-epinephrine by inhibiting reuptake at the synapse (Carter, 2002, p.102).

Other drugs were later introduced and, most interestingly, drugs usually designed for those who suffer from schizophrenia or Bipolar Disorder became widely used by those who suffer with depression. This is a strange phenomenon. If we have definite categories of the "illness", such as schizophrenia, bipolar, or depression, why do we give one medication (Seroquel, for example) to treat the three different conditions?

Hittman and Zuckerman write that:

> ...Seroquel is widely prescribed for patients who could be treated at least as effectively with safer, less expensive medication. Consumers need to be their own advocates because even if a prescription drug label warns to try other medication first, many doctors tend to overlook this warning... the risks are too great. These side effects are considered acceptable for schizophrenia treatment, but should not be considered acceptable for depression or anxiety, since there are other, safer alternatives (2009, p:2).

Hittman and Zuckerman (2009) further argue that in 2006, Seroquel was AstraZeneca's second biggest moneymaker, with sales over $3 billion. What is strange is that this drug is indicated for people who suffer from schizophrenia and should not be given to people who suffer from anxiety or depression because of the dangerous side effects which, in some cases, can lead to the development of tardive dyskinesia[5] and cardiovascular problems including, on rare occasions, heart attack.

Seroquel was introduced to the US market as a second-generation antipsychotic drug and while it became one of the biggest sellers, its side effects were serious and sometimes deadly. These side effects can include: neuroleptic malignant syndrome, fatal instances of heatstroke, cataracts, and tardive dyskinesia, which is a lifelong condition with no known effective cures.

On rare occasion, in the early stages of the disorder, tardive dyskinesia can be reversed. It is helpful to add here that I, who suffers from Bipolar Disorder, was once on Seroquel. I developed early symptoms of tardive dyskinesia and was forced to gradually reduce the dose till I stopped taking the medication. For many months, I was left with severe headaches and a general feeling of being extremely dizzy, but I was fortunate not to develop tardive dyskinesia. The interesting thing is that I was only on a small dose.

It was also found, more alarmingly, that women who switched from first generation to second generation antipsychotic drugs, such as Seroquel, were at an increased risk for unwanted pregnancies. Recently there have been a number of court cases against the company Astra Zeneca because of the serious side effects of Seroquel and the fact that many patients have developed life-threatening illnesses, or even died. Croning Fisk (2007) writes:

> "AstraZeneca PLC, the U.K.'s second-largest drug maker, has been sued by almost 10,000 people in the U.S. over claimed injuries from defects in the company's antipsychotic drug Seroquel, according to a court filing. Patients claim in their complaints that AstraZeneca didn't adequately warn of possible side effects, including severe weight gain and risk of diabetes. Many of the suits contend the London- based company and its affiliates promoted the drug for unapproved uses, contrary to U.S. Food and Drug Administration regulations."

All the hype and publicity of the second-generation psychotic drugs was based on advertising and often false presentation of the efficacy of the newer drugs, which in many cases had worse side effects than first-generation antipsychotic drugs. Among patients with schizophrenia whose medication is changed because of ineffectiveness or harmful side effects, second-generation antipsychotic drugs do not appear to offer significant

---

[5] *Tardive dyskinesia* is a disorder that involves involuntary movements, especially of the lower face. Usually untreatable and may involve extremities as well.

benefits compared to first-generation antipsychotic drugs. The findings run contrary to the widely held perception that second-generation antipsychotic agents are safer and more effective in treating patients with schizophrenia than the less-expensive first-generation class of medications (Lancet, 2009).

What makes it even stranger is the fact that it is well-known that antidepressants cannot be given to people who are experiencing mania because to do so would further fuel the mania. A person who suffers with Bipolar finds her or himself confronted by this dilemma as depression and mania alternate.

But how do antipsychotic drugs work? The vast majority of antipsychotics work by blocking the absorption of dopamine, a chemical that occurs naturally in the brain and is responsible for causing psychotic reactions...

> "Dopamine is one of the substances in the brain responsible for transmitting messages across the gaps, or synapses, of nerve cells. Too much dopamine in a person's brain speeds up nerve impulses to the point of causing hallucinations, delusions, and thought disorders. By blocking the dopamine receptors, antipsychotics reduce the severity of these symptoms" (American Psychiatry Association, 1993).

The brain has several types of dopamine receptors, and their unselective blockage by antipsychotic drugs causes the side effects. The belief is that when a patient takes an antipsychotic drug, he or she enters what is called a neuroleptic state. Impulsiveness and aggression decrease as do concerns and arousal about events going on in the environment outside the person. The person taking the drugs has fewer hallucinations and delusions as well. Once these symptoms are controlled by antipsychotic drugs, he or she can live a more normal life, and physicians can more easily treat the cause of the psychosis (Buelow and Herbert, 1995).

Perhaps it is possible that decreasing the amount of dopamine is beneficial for all mental disorders but, given that we still know so very little about how the brain really works, it is plausible to think that serious consequences for humanity may be in the cards, not to mention the sometimes devastating side effects which can be worse than the mental disorder.

The question that comes to mind is: are there any other methods, apart from psychiatric drugs, to help sufferers without affecting their health because of dangerous side effects and derived illnesses? The placebo effect may also explain why medication is effective, even though we don't fully understand how or why it works. For example, psychologist Dr Robert Rich writes:

> "One of the standard things is that a GP prescribes a drug that has a lead time of say a week before it becomes effective. The patient reports immediate relief. This does not mean that the drug is no good or unnecessary, but it *is* the placebo effect. This term is a rather dismissive way of describing the wonderful healing powers of the mind. I have a painful shoulder at the moment. I went to a physiotherapist, who encouraged me to do exercises. This didn't seem to help much, so I went to another bloke, who told me to keep it as still as possible, and avoid aggravating it. You know what? The pain levels *increased*. Then I went for an ultrasound, which showed the complete tear of a muscle. The doctor said, "You can do whatever you like. It's stuffed, you can't damage it anymore." Since then, the pain levels have *decreased*. It's all in how you think about things."

The other interesting phenomenon is that some people do not benefit from medication at all. For example, this sufferer wrote to me in an email exchange:

> "Overall, looking back over my life of many years... I've had years and years on meds and I've had years and years off meds. I see very little to no difference. I struggle and suffer with the debilitating effects and affects of my mental illness. Yet, I keep getting up when my mind shouts *lay down and die*, and I keep stepping forward, though more and more stumbling and falling face down. Still, I get back up."

She was not alone because I found, from personal research, that many of my correspondents did not benefit from antidepressants or antipsychotic drugs. I would say that about 40% of correspondents, to give a very rough estimate, either took no medication or found the medication useless. This sufferer, Michael, wrote:

> "They haven't done anything for me except add 100+ lbs, add impotence, and other symptoms that I'm convinced were caused by the pills, and yadda yadda yadda.... I thought they were supposed to make my life better."

And again this sufferer, Poppy, in an email exchange writes about her struggle with seriously dangerous side effects of the drug Efferox XL. In regard to this, she writes:

"The Effexor XL was given to me when I had successfully come off Paxil [We call it Seroxat] after 20 years. I did it myself and I did very well. However, 3 months later, coming up to Xmas, I came down with an awful depression. The psychiatrist put me on Effexor XL; this was nearly 7years ago. I became worse and eventually I was on an extremely high dose, over 250 mg, which is above recommended dose. I had a T.I.A. some years ago and told the psychiatrist I was seeing [in the public Medical hospital] that I was feeling Dizzy and felt my BP was up. I have NEVER suffered from high BP in my life. She took my blood pressure and it was very high, so she panicked and took me down a lot on the Effexor.

I decided to do some 'homework' myself on the Effexor XL and to look at some scholarly reports rather than the Drug Companies' information. I was appalled to note that the side effects were all the things that had happened to me for the *first time* in my life: High Cholesterol, High Blood Pressure, Agitation, Obesity, Carbohydrate Craving. I had not had any of the above in my life before taking the drug. I also was very angry to read that the drug was Recommended For Use Mainly When All Other Antidepressants Had Failed !!

I was very angry at this as I hadn't been put on any other anti-depressants or failed to respond. I had simply decided to try and live my life without SSRIs or antidepressants, staying on a small amount of sedation and a sleeping pill when needed. Looking back, I believe that the depression was probably induced by the fact that after 20 years, I was still suffering from withdrawals and my own chemicals hadn't started working properly; i.e., the neurons were used to being boosted with Serotonin etc. I know that it has been proven that SSRIs leave the brain sites after 14 days but I still think their effects are on a different level; maybe these effects cannot be picked up on an MRI or other scan but the brain definitely has trouble getting back to normal after being on them for 20 years. *back to the effexor...* When I asked the Professor at my hospital to titrate me down from the Effexor, he refused; he said that it was a very good drug and that I was doing very well on it.

I didn't think I was doing well on it. I found it very addictive. Whilst titrating down from the very high dose, I'd gone through awful withdrawals, much worse than the Seroxat. I felt 'spaced out'; I didn't have much empathy. I would watch sad things but not feel sad in my heart. I felt nothing... not high, not low, not gay, or happy except perhaps for very brief moments. I was a chemical zombie in some ways. I also lost my sexuality completely and had become very fat.

I had to ask and ask and eventually, I started to titrate myself. My prof. said I was 'very silly to do it' when they agreed with me!!! He knew of the blood pressure and the cholesterol. He only agreed that I'd have to come off when my MD said I was a 'walking time bomb'.

My GP [doctor] said he couldn't understand why I had been put on this drug and that he and his colleagues never used it. He urged me to insist that my psychiatrist titrate me down off it. And so I did. I can't say I got any help whatsoever; in fact, the psychiatrist said it was possible I'd 'CRASH' and if I did, he'd be happy to put me back on the Effexor.

I had to hide how awful I was feeling. My depression intensified and the withdrawals were unbearable and ongoing. Eventually I came off and went slowly onto the Lexapro. I asked him to put me on Lexapro as I had studied the SSRIs and it seemed the best. My General Practitioner said to me that Lexapro was a 'cleaner' drug."

What does the latest research tell us about antidepressants and antipsychotic drugs? Linford and Arden inform that one important research has revealed that psychiatric medication may not be as efficient as promoted by the pharmaceutical companies through the media. They mention a study conducted by Turner, Matthews, Linardatos, Tell & Rosenthal (2008).

These researchers "subpoenaed the US government to release all the studies on antidepressants ' effectiveness in its archives." (Linford & Arden 2009, p:19). What was found was that there were many studies disputing the hypothesis that SSRIs are more effective than placebos. More interestingly, research papers in favor of the positive effects of anti-depressants were twelve times more likely to be published than studies reporting negative results. Turner et.al (2008), in the study, concluded that:

> Publications' bias had inflated the common impression of the effectiveness of serotonin reuptake inhibitors by about a third overall; and for some medications, the figures were twice as high. Post-Turner estimates of the effects of antidepressants have dropped to a level close to that of placebo (Linford and Arden 2009, pp :19-20).

Despite the many research papers which clearly indicate that the Western world has over estimated the effectiveness of antidepressants or psychotic drugs, huge amounts of prescriptions continue to be written every year and the numbers increase steadily and dramatically.

Professor of Statistics at the Australian Macquarie University, John S. Croucher (2003), stated that "the number of prescriptions written for antidepressant drugs in Australia in 2002 was 9 million, in 1996, 2.7 million". Today the statistical number is much higher than 9 million prescription drugs. It is clear that there are huge profits made by pharmaceutical companies. It could be said that drug companies are aware of the money-making potential and have helped push the increase by encouraging doctors to write unnecessary prescriptions.

In a research on the antidepressant Imipramine, it was found that the drug was more effective than placebo. In the study reanalysis, the result was very different as the conclusion was that the most effective psychiatrist actually achieved better results with placebo than the worst-performing psychiatrist achieved with antidepressants (McKay, Zac & Wampold, 2006).

The research seems to indicate that it is important to be cautious when writing research on the effectiveness of drugs because it would seem that we have been affected by a dominant and unhelpful ideology that drugs alone can help in the control of mental disorders. Moreover, many sufferers are given a number of medications, sometimes as is the case in America, up to seven different prescription drugs for the same mental disorder such as bipolar, for example. This is what Edward, a sufferer from America, writes: "...for my Bipolar Disorder, I take Lamictal, Adderall, Seroquel, Abilify, Effexor and Klonopin."

Such a witches' brew, particularly without knowing the effects of mixing these dangerous drugs, should not be permitted by a responsible society. Such concoction of drugs is not desirable because there are no studies on the interaction of drugs, particularly dangerous ant psychotic drugs. In some instances, drugs may be indicated when a patient is experiencing psychosis and needs help to regain control of his thoughts and actions.

Recently, science is beginning to tell us that we need to promote psychotherapy and attempt to reduce antipsychotic and antidepressant drugs because, as statistics show, a huge increase in the number of sufferers is ringing alarm bells. This may lead to an important question: are we creating mental illness in our society? For example, Robert Whitaker (in Messman, 2005) argues that antipsychotic medication and antidepressants, while used when they should not be, have created a drug-induced epidemic of real mental illness since the drugs affect the brain directly.

There are numerous professionals and commentators who support Whitaker's perspective. For example, Dr Whitfield (2010, abstract) writes:

> ...Drawing on the work of numerous psychiatrists and psychopharmacologists and my own observation, I describe how most common psychiatric drugs are not only toxic but can be chronically traumatic, which I define in some details throughout this paper. In addition to observing this occurrence amongst numerous of my patients over the past 20 years, I surveyed 9 mental health clinicians who had taken antidepressant drugs long-term. Of these 9, 7 (78%) experienced bothersome toxic drug effects and 2 (22%) had become clearly worse than they were before they started the drugs. Based on others' and my observations, I describe the genesis of this worsened condition which I call the Drug-Stress Trauma Syndrome.

Psychiatric medication can sometimes save lives by bringing back manic patient down to reality, using massive doses of medication. Nevertheless, I think that psychiatric medication should be treated as a temporary intervention in exceptional cases.

We are becoming increasingly aware, looking at the various literature and research, that psychiatric medication is not indicated in many instances. Unfortunately the current trend is to overmedicate as many people as possible. Because of the ideology of mental illness as biological illness, many people have learned to rely heavily on psychiatric medication with serious consequences.

Drugs may be indicated where therapy has failed due to the nature of the sufferer who may be unable to open up or benefit from therapy for whatever reason. It is well known that therapy does not work for everyone. But therapy can work well for many people and there should be an effort to use talk therapy, mindfulness activities and other natural methods first. Drugs should never be the first choice and should only be administered keeping in mind that the least dose possible that brings improvement is the best way to go. Antidepressants and antipsychotic drugs are a crutch. Some people may need them for life, but others can learn to walk without them.

It is true to say that many sufferers with bipolar and other mental disorders who are creative, especially performing artists, are often afraid to take antipsychotics for fear that these will reduce or even undermine their creativity. Stephen Fry is one of these gifted artists who has publically spoken about this concern of his. Of course for us, who suffer with Bipolar II or Cyclothymia, which is known as "bipolar light", it is possible to cope with little or no medication while benefitting from the wonderful feelings of highs and lows, which seem to fuel the creativity. But for those with more severe conditions, it is not this simple and medication is often a must. Because of this, I now include two essays I wrote to do with the link between mental and physical disorders and creativity.

Creativity and the Creative Artist

It is extremely difficult to write about creativity, and it is just as difficult to explore the relationship between creativity and the mind. In addition, what is defined or identified as creativity and what is not depends very much on context; therefore, creativity is context-dependent. So where do we start?

Universals do exist and this is precisely what makes the study of creativity so very interesting. Rather than develop an argument that will follow a certain sequence, I will offer separate discussions of what I, as a creative artist, in communication with many other artists, have come to understand about creativity. However, the discussion is not completely subjective because I will give references to academic ideas about the creative process that either support or refute the commentator's perspectives.

Amongst various commentators, there is the belief that artists are unable to give an adequate explanation of their creative process. Ask an artist what goes on in their mind during the creative process and they will give a variety of very unusual answers, such as saying that their creative ideas come from an outside source separate from them and their mind, and that they are in tune with this source, just like a receiver and a transmitter. Such unusual explanations are very common amongst artists, as I will discuss in parts of this journal. What are we to make out of these explanations? Are artists simply ignorant? And why do they fail to adhere to the academic explanations of what is going on during the creative process?

As a creative and multi-talented artist, I am aware of this problem. I will develop an argument to show that the reason artists are unable to explain their creative process in such a way that the explanation makes sense to the academia is because the academic discourse is missing important information that has been disregarded and that is the science of "heart intelligence".

Current research shows that the human heart is now recognized by scientists as a highly complex system with its own inbuilt brain[6]. While many commentators argue that the heart brain has only about 40,000 neuron cells (and therefore, this is not enough for the heart to be significantly intelligent), some evidence tells a different story. There are documented cases of heart transplant recipients who, after the transplant, have suddenly become accomplished artists and others who have taken on personality characteristics of their donors.

This would tend to indicate that heart intelligence is involved in the creative process. Moreover, we have to keep in mind that the human heart can live up to 16 hours out of the body and that it has a magnetic field which is 5000 times (or "units") stronger, in amplitude, than the human brain. Much research also shows that the heart intelligence is somehow involved in premonition and other unexplained phenomena. While academics are keeping a distance from this kind of research, for an artist like me, heart intelligence makes a lot of sense and I will discuss why. I feel that heart intelligence can be used to make sense of the way in which artists describe their creative process. Without a doubt, this is the area of research which will lead us to great scientific understandings of creativity.

Creativity, according to the *Oxford Companion to the Mind* (1987), is the use of the imagination or original ideas, especially in the production of an artistic work. That is, it's not the production of certain results such as music, art or scientific theories, but the mental process that leads to such products. It is a way of life. A highly creative person behaves, thinks and acts in ways imbued by the relevant set of characteristics.

Creativity is a term that is not one single human characteristic, but one that directs us to a number of concerns that are quite separate: innovation and discoveries refer to ideas and objects that people produce; self-actualization refers to the quality of life a person leads; imagination and fantasy refer to what goes on inside a person's head (ibid).

Creativity is context-dependent. This means that to be creative, a product or idea must have meaning both to creator and to her or his audience (Rothenberg 1994, Boden 2004); and we also have to consider that meaning is not fixed but that it can change in time. A good example and evidence of the validity of these two statements can be found if we look at the life of Vincent van Gogh. He was a great artist but during his lifetime his paintings were not recognized by the world; for a variety of reasons, some known and some unknown, his paintings were considered

[6] http://www.in5d.com/heart-has-brain-and-consciousness.html

to be a departure from what was acceptable in his time. In this sense, the paintings had meaning to the creator but not to the world. Later, and this is proof that meaning changes, his paintings became accepted as great works of art. Today van Gogh's work is recognized as great art. Meaning for his paintings has been found, but only after his death.

Because creativity is dependent on meaning, it is subjective, and any attempt to define it objectively will be flawed. For example, we can look at the creative work of Duchamp titled "Fountain" (1917) where he submitted a urinal to an art exhibition. The urinal was signed and dated. The idea is certainly creative. Who would have thought to sign a urinal and call it a piece of creative art? In addition, there are lots of related concepts that can be attached to the meaning of this work. Some critics accept Duchamp's "Fountain" as a work of art, while others don't. The creative act is subject to whether it is recognized as creative art or not. The fact that a work can be judged as creative by one generation and defined as rubbish by another generation is proof of the subjective nature of creativity. The work of van Gogh can again be taken as an example: it was considered rubbish in his generation and valued as wonderfully creative in our generation.

To avoid the problems that derive from the context dependency of creativity, we could proceed to break down context into smaller units of enquiry. We could start by taking into consideration the creator and attempt to study what the work meant or means to the creator. This is not to say that creativity is not subjective, but that at least we can begin to get a better picture of the creative process. In this sense, we do admit that creativity is subjective, but we also realize that this does not make it impossible for us to study the creative process. We can further break down the individual creative process into originality of the work, which would require an observation and identification of the divergent thought.

Divergent thinking is a thought process (unusual and unstereotyped) used to generate creative ideas to explore many possible solutions to a problem. It is a process that happens in a free-flowing and spontaneous manner. In some cases, as in my case, it can happen at the subconscious level and then be brought up to the conscious when I least expect it. I feel that heart intelligence is also involved in this process and I will explain why I think this is so in the heart intelligence section in this book. In the next section, I deal with the creative person and his society and look at how the outer world interacts with creative people.

Our society is organized to suppress creativity. Even with advances in education practices, young children in school are required to conform, to approach learning activities in ways set out by the curriculum and to cooperate with the teacher and other children who do not share the child's unique ways of thinking. In regard to this, a sufferer (S8) who is one of the subjects of my personal longitudinal research, sent this interesting comment:

> "Have you ever read John Holt's writing? He wrote some great books and a wonderful newsletter for several years, before he passed away, about 'un-schooling' (homeschooling where the child leads the agenda according to his interests and capabilities). I homeschooled my children using his methods for several years until I found a private school that did foster creativity and did not promote conformity. This was quite a few years ago, as my children are now 32 and 29, so these newsletters were published at least 20 plus years ago!! These issues have been addressed very well in these newsletters, so I hope you will be able to get some copies of them."

Certainly, John Holt's writings were a very powerful critique of modern education. In an interview, he comments that:

> ...children do poorly in school because they're bored with the meaningless work... scared of being punished or humiliated... and confused by the fact that most teaching progresses from abstract concepts to concrete examples instead of the opposite as would be more sensible the other way around. In essence I'd realized, from observing and teaching, that school is a place where children *learn* to be stupid! ...I suggested we simply provide young people with schools where there are a lot of interesting things to look at and work with... but that we let the children learn in their own ways. If they have questions, answer the questions. If they want to know where to look for something, show them where to look (Holt: 1980).

In other words, children should be active participants in their learning. The creative mind learns by doing in practical terms, just like Holt describes, from the concrete to the abstract and not the other way around.

There have been many writers who have written extensively about education as the tool for social reproduction and maintenance of the oppressive and unjust status quo. Some of these famous commentators are: Ivan Illich (1972), Robert Disch, R.D. Laing (1967), A.S. Neill (1983), and Paolo Freire (1970).' Freire, in his book, *Pedagogy of the Oppressed*, describes the education process as a banking system and he writes:

...Education thus becomes an act of depositing, in which the students are the depositories and the teacher is the depositor. Instead of communicating, the teacher issues communiqués and makes deposits, which the students patiently receive, memorize, and repeat. This is the "banking" concept of education, in which the scope of action allowed to the students extends only as far as receiving, filing, and storing the deposits"[a description that brings to mind the modern computer or the mind mimicking the computer] (1970: 56-7).

By definition, creative people are imaginative and original. This makes them act differently from others while the pressure from most parents, teachers, and certainly from peer groups, is to conform, to copy, to act like everyone else in the group.

People who are creative, therefore, are often unable to function to their fullest potential because our society requires that we conform to prescribed rules and ideologies. This is something necessary; but in our world, there is pressure to avoid being different; the odd one out is likely to be victimized, exploited, or treated with ridicule. Hence, I claim that creativity in our society is largely suppressed. In support of this, counseling expert Connie Eales wrote:

But to whom do parents go if they suspect that their infant or toddler is intellectually advanced or possesses exceptional talent? A psychologist? But people usually go to see a psychologist or a 'shrink' only if they are slightly 'emotionally disturbed' to use the dreaded label. No wonder parents who suspect that their child is talented will pretend they have not noticed anything and hope that 'maybe it will go away' (Eales 1983:2).

The creative person will always suffer the creative anguish, but creative suppression makes it all that much harder to cope. The creative process often involves joy. All the same, it is also full of anguish. When caught up in the act of creation, a child is likely to be short-tempered, distracted, and unable to perform everyday tasks or keep to routines. This often leads to disapproval from authority figures and hostility from peers.

The creative person who suffers from creative anguish is often a student of the human condition. In my personal research, I found that many artists are concerned with the human environment. This is certainly true of many artists of the past, such as Picasso or van Gogh. Caring for people and the world and the study of the human condition are often the concerns of a good artist. Picasso had a message which was read by a nurse and transmitted by phone to the American Artists Congress back in 1937. He expressed the following thoughts:

> "I always believed and believe that the artists who live and work according to spiritual values cannot and should not remain indifferent to the conflict in which the highest values of the humanity and the civilization are in game" (Picasso: 1937).

The artist who lives and works according to spiritual values will realize, at one point, that humanity is experiencing a kind of spiritual bankruptcy. Danah Zohar writes that:

> The beginning of the 21st century... is associated in the West by selfishness, materialism, a lack of morals, a lack of value, lack of sense of community and, ultimately, lack of meaning. This affects rich and poor alike (Zorah: 2000).

This situation describes a spiritual and intellectual environment that is not really suitable for highly creative people. For example, talented and gifted individuals will find it hard to fit in society, despite the efforts of educators, psychologists, and scientists who try to make room for the brightest and most creative individuals. This is because the problems are deep into the structures of our social organization. Pearl Buck wrote the following about talented and gifted individuals:

> "The truly creative mind in any field is no more than this: A human creature born abnormally, inhumanly sensitive. To him... a touch is a blow, a sound is a noise, a misfortune is a tragedy, a joy is an ecstasy, a friend is a lover, a lover is a god, and failure is death. Add to this cruelly delicate organism the overpowering necessity to create, create, create... so that without the creating of music or poetry or books or buildings or something of meaning, his very breath is cut off from him. He must create, must pour out creation. By some strange, unknown, inward urgency, he is not really alive unless he is creating" (Berger: 2009).

Highly creative individuals are open to ideas and are both emotionally and intellectually sensitive. This, in the world in which we live today, is a disability in itself. It makes sense to deduce from this that both people who suffer with mental illness and those who are extremely talented or gifted experience stigma and are often unable to live a fully productive life. To be talented or gifted is to suffer to a point where the suffering becomes a disability (ibid).

There have been many attempts to define creativity and to come up with ways to test it. My personal research is based on emails sent to me by hundreds of people from all over the world. These emails provide a pool of ideas and conceptualizations about what creativity is and a way to analyze the relevant variables. Some of these aspects include the product created, the personality of the creator, the environment's influence, and the level of heart intelligence, which is much more than just rational intelligence measurable in IQ tests. Such intelligence has to do with sensitivity, feelings, emotions, lateral thinking, and divergent thinking to name a few.

Because of its inherent variability and uniqueness, creativity is difficult to categorize and, therefore, doesn't easily yield itself to statistical analysis. Fortunately, in recent years, qualitative analysis has gained respectability.

To be defined as "creative," in a particular field, one needs to have a good well of knowledge to draw from; but at the same time, one must be able to work outside of the rigidity of knowledge that often accompanies the expert who knows her subject too thoroughly.

Intelligence and coherence must be present but, at the same time, this has to be connected to the divergent thinking which, in turn, leads to creative ideas.

As an artist, I remember feeling the urge to paint something unusual about humanity, greed in particular. I was aware of Picasso's painting "Guernica", which is what inspired my painting titled *For the Love of Money*. At that time, I felt that something terrible was going to happen, a historical event that would be remembered for a very long time. This feeling was right; my premonition proved to be correct. I am not making this up because a copy of the painting was given to the counselor of my university, just a year or so before the events of September 11, when two planes flew into the Twin Towers of the World Trade Center in America. Nearly 3000 people died as a consequence. I was not aware of where, when, or who would be affected, but I knew that many people would lose their lives. I include two versions of the painting on the following pages:

"For the Love of Money" (Version A)
Drawing by Alfredo Zotti, 2000

"For the Love of Money" (Version B)
Drawing by Alfredo Zotti, 2000

What is different about the painting is that it is done in the style of a cartoon and yet, the figures resemble Picasso's style: we see two eyes on the same side of the face and all sorts of similar irregularities that are a departure from the normal way of portraying people and which were the trademark of Picasso. Yet this painting is not Picasso's style. It is an original style unlike any other. Original thought is never totally unique in that it relies on objects and ideas that have already been done or thought of or written about. But it is a reformulation of these objects or ideas that makes the work original. In this sense, creativity, originality, and art are subject to cultural context because they are expressions of language, meaning, and symbols that are reformulated into novel ways of doing things.

Any original idea is part of the creative process. In this sense, I totally disagree with some commentators who argue that originality is not always creativity. Mothers who find new ways of coping with their children or workers who find unusual and creative ways to get the job done better and more quickly are creative people who engage in divergent thinking and use it to come up with novel ways of doing things or solving problems. This is creativity, at least for me.

Creativity is complex. For example, one day I needed to put all of my business cards in some order, and I was looking for something to hold the ones which I use the most. At the same time, I was looking at a cassette case, one of those old cassette tapes of the 1970s and 80s.

I took the cover and the tape out and I was left with the plastic shell, which I positioned in such a way that it was now a business card holder. For me, this is creativity, as well; and if I were to place this card holder in an art exhibition, it could be considered to be a work of art. In this case, it is the *idea* that represents the artistic work, not the material itself. I include a picture of the card holder on the next page.

A 1980s style plastic cassette holder.

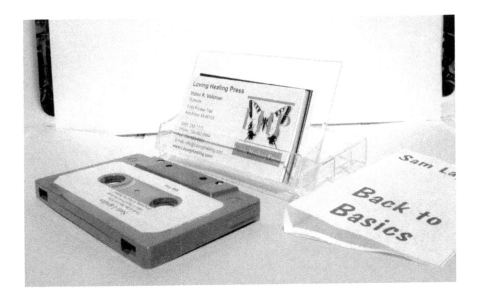

The shell of an old tape cassette is now a business card holder.

Some of the characteristics of creativity are now beginning to surface. I will attempt to list some of the main characteristics of the creative process.

As I have previously argued, the creative product needs to be both original and have meaning. Commentators like Mihaly Csikszentmihalyi (1998) propose that creativity depends on social context and it is only the context-value judgment that can be studied. This idea does make sense, but it is too rigid a way to describe creativity, a process which is para-doxical, at best. Generally speaking, art and creativity are context-dependent, but there are exceptions to the rules. For example, below is a painting that was exhibited in an art gallery and received much attention, although it was not the winning painting. Nevertheless, it came in third.

My representational art is not as creative as my abstract art, at least for me. It is more of a technical set of skills although, admittedly, there is also need for some creativity. The following pages include some of the portraits that I have made over the years.

"The Face of Depression" (my father)
Drawing by Alfredo Zotti

Portrait of a Dog

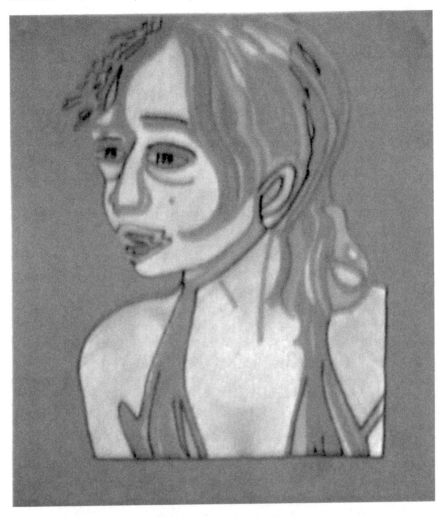

Portrait of Agnes

There is, however, a way to paint a portrait which is much more creative than conventional representation. Above is a portrait of my cousin, Agnes, which came to me in a dream. The colored hair and the Picasso style of placing eyes and facial features in a sort of fourth dimensional manner, possibly inspired by my synesthesia, is what gives this painting its unique characteristic. It is a fact that creative people often get their creative ideas from dreams, or when they least expect it, while doing something completely irrelevant to the idea. I feel this is also linked to heart intelligence.

The link between creativity and mental illness is well-established in research. Research shows that creativity and mental illness share a common set of traits. Simonton (2004), Post (1996), and Peterson, Smith, and Carsons (2002) argue that creators will commonly exhibit symptoms often associated with mental illness. A new study suggests that Bipolar Disorder (but also other types of mental illness) and creativity actually share a common root (New Scientist, 29 October, p.40). My longitudinal research supports this claim. The most common traits found in the creative mental anguish cases are mood swings, particularly what we call unipolar and Bipolar Disorder and, of course, anxiety of a level diagnosable as a disorder is also very frequent.

Current research findings point to a clear link between the gene called *neuregulin 1* (NRG1) and creativity. These are some of the research findings[7]:

> Vincent van Gogh cut off his ear. Sylvia Plath stuck her head in the oven. History teems with examples of great artists acting in very peculiar ways. Were these artists simply mad, or were they brilliant? According to new research reported in *Psychological Science*, a journal of the Association for Psychological Science, maybe both.
>
> In order to examine the link between psychosis and creativity, psychiatrist Szabolcs Kéri of Semmelweis University in Hungary focused his research on neuregulin 1, a gene that normally plays a role in a variety of brain processes, including development and strengthening communication between neurons. However, a variant of this gene (or genotype) is associated with a greater risk of developing mental disorders, such as schizophrenia and Bipolar Disorder.
>
> In this study, the researchers recruited volunteers who considered themselves to be very creative and accomplished. They underwent a battery of tests, including assessments for intelligence and creativity. To measure creativity, the volunteers were asked to respond to a series of unusual questions (for example, "Just suppose clouds had strings attached to them which hang down to earth. What would happen?") and were scored based on the originality and flexibility of their answers. They also completed a questionnaire regarding their lifetime creative achievements before the researchers took blood samples.

---

[7] https://www.psychologicalscience.org/media/releases/2009/keri.cfm

The results show a clear link between neuregulin 1 and creativity. Volunteers with the specific variant of this gene were more likely to have higher scores on the creativity assessment and also greater lifetime creative achievements than volunteers with a different form of the gene. Kéri notes that this is the first study to show that a genetic variant associated with psychosis may have some beneficial functions. He observes that "molecular factors that are loosely associated with severe mental disorders but are present in many healthy people may have an advantage enabling us to think more creatively." In addition, these findings suggest that certain genetic variations, even though associated with adverse health problems, may survive evolutionary selection and remain in a population's gene pool if they also have beneficial effects (APS Press Release, 28 September 2009).

It is important to acknowledge that mild forms of mental illness, such as depression, anxiety, cyclothymia, or Bipolar II, are ideal in terms of creative output. Severe symptoms can hinder the creative process and, indeed, it is unthinkable to suggest that a person who is experiencing full mania or severe chronic depression could engage in the creative process. In this sense, it is usually those with milder symptoms who can cope and have a creative career that lasts. An example of such individuals is actor Stephen Fry, who suffers with bipolar 2 and also has synesthesia.

Mild to moderate depression seems to be the force that propels the creative drive, although many artists argue against this idea. In my longitudinal research, I have found that many people, like me, are at their most creative when they experience moderate depression. For example, here is what one sufferer (S14) writes, which is representative of many subjects of my longitudinal research:

"I have found since early childhood that I am at my most creative, really deeply creative, when I'm deeply depressed; I can throw something out when 'up' but it's when I'm at my darkest sometimes that the most stirring words and/or images come out. It is as if the pain, or even that last hope sometimes, is worked through the words that are spoken and/or typed, or the image I sketch. Folks and teachers have, on the spot, insisted on me sketching or writing and I've always had trouble doing so. It has been hard. When I'm up, as you said, the ideas are spinning so fast that it is hard to hold onto one long enough to really see it through or follow the train of thought in writing or speaking."

This seems to be contrary to what Kay Jamison (1993) proposes. She writes that it is hypomania which is the most creative of moods and which is associated with creative production. One of the books that I have found to be most interesting, about the link between mental anguish and creativity, is *Touched With Fire* (1993) by Kay Jamison, who is a professor of psychiatry at the Johns Hopkins University School of Medicine. This book seems to me to be directed at the non-professional audience, perhaps to sufferers directly, and as such, it is entertaining and instructive. It is a book written by a professional who suffers directly. Kay Jamison states that she suffers from Manic Depression, or what is also known as Bipolar Disorder.

Nevertheless, the book, like all books, is not free from problems. One of the biggest problems for me is that she often addresses sufferers as "manic" or "depressives", which tends to promote a conceptualization of people as disease states or "cases." In regard to this, a sufferer (S12) once wrote to me the following and I include it here at the risk of going off on a tangent away from the discussion, even if for a moment:

"I don't know if this applies but I have always found it disheartening that if you take someone diagnosed with Bipolar, who may or may not be on meds, is reasonably stable by following their own path of treatment and therapy (not all forms of Bipolar require pharmaceutical medication or not quite as much), as soon as they express some type of idea that 'normal' society deems a bit odd, they are advised 'to go see your doc because you might need a tweak or you may want to discuss getting on a medication for that.' They feel down because well… they feel down, or lost a job, or had surgery, or a friend moved away [and] immediately someone suggests 'to go see your doc because you might need a tweak or you may want to discuss getting on a medication for that.' That person isn't allowed to be *human*. I am not saying that all with Bipolar do not need intensive medication therapy, because based on the severity of the illness to that individual, intensive medication may very well be warranted.

However, I think it rather sad when fellow patients with the disorder, professional staff treating those with the disorder, and/ or family members of the ones with the disorder, just won't let the one with the disorder be allowed to experience normal human emotions or ideas without everyone jumping on them to have a medication added, tweaked, adjusted, started, and / or dropped. It's also sad that when one who has struggled with the illness, has gone the traditional route, has undergone therapy for years, decides to cut back on their meds or try some alternative form of therapy because nothing else has helped or is helping, rather than be supported, are judged and criticized and accused of being irresponsible, even by fellow patients with the disorder."

Getting back on track now, I want to focus on Kay Jamison's idea that it is the hypomania, in Bipolar Disorder, that is mostly associated with creative production; conversely, during depression, the sufferer experiences lethargy and hopelessness and is creatively unproductive.

Certainly, there is some truth in Kay Jamison's idea of productive hypomanic moods versus non-productive depressive moods. From my research, however, I find the situation to be much more complex as each person's experiences of moods and what they can do within these moods/states is as unique as the person. Each person is a Universe in her or his own right.

There was a noticeable creative productivity of musical works during Shumann's hypomanic states, while there is a very marked decrease in productivity and sometimes an absence of productivity during his depression. There could be a number of reasons for this. It is quite possible that Shumann was most creative while experiencing hypomania. Also, Shumann's era was one in which many artists and affluent people used opium to cope with many health problems and often drank alcohol abusively. Moreover, Shumann suffered from syphilis and took various drugs for this condition, including mercury, which can have a devastating effect on brain function and the nervous system and which would have certainly affected or worsened his moods and mental anguish. However, we cannot use the example of Shumann's hypomanic productivity to broadly state that it is hypomania, in Bipolar Disorder, that is the most creative and productive period of a sufferer. This would not accurately explain my experience of Bipolar Disorder as an artist.

To support her argument, Kay Jamison discusses the productive and non-productive life of Robert Shumann:

> "While some cases of mild hypomania may lead to creative output, and I know this because I suffer with hypomania, it seems that depression is the mood most associated with my creativity. This is an idea that is supported by much literature and autobiographies of many creative people. Paul Redfield (1993) wrote, "Wherever one went the world was blossoming. And yet despair gave birth to poetry."

I am also a composer and a pianist, as well as having many other artistic talents, and I also suffer with the so-called Bipolar Disorder. While the output of my creative productivity varies by periods, I cannot claim to be most creative during hypomanic moods. I may be more productive while hypomanic but, for me, the real creative genius derives from my creative anguish, which is neither depression nor hypomania, but a kind of depressive reflection on life—best described as artistic anguish. This is because if I were experiencing hypomania proper, I would not be able to achieve much, since my mind would be all over the place and I would not be able to focus enough to produce anything of substance. In regard to this, S5 writes:

> "When I am hypomanic I am unable to do anything because my mind shifts from one idea to the next and I cannot get anything done."

Similarly, I would not be able to create much if I were to suffer deep depression of the sort that had me confined to my bed for days. In regard to this, S12, who suffers from Unipolar Depression, writes:

> "Well, I can't speak about mania from personal experience, but my creativity is dampened when I am down. No energy to bother with anything."

And again, creativity is very personal and the creative process is not the same for all people. For example, S12, who is a very creative person, writes:

> "This is interesting, and very different from my personal experience. My creativity is in top gear when I forget that I as a person even exist, and am fully involved in the task. It then flows of its own accord. When I am writing like this, I don't feel I own the words. I am merely a conduit for them. They come through me, not from me."

In support of this view, S13 writes:

> "It is out of mindfulness that creativity arises. When one is in the act of creation, they are immersed in the moment, observing what is now. They are not thinking about yesterday, tomorrow, or in judgment of their actions; they are flowing with the creation; they are the creation, one with it, not concerned with the action or the outcome. They may stop to reflect on what they have created. I am not driven to create I cannot relate it to a mood or a state of mind, rather it is better described as a state

of no mind or observance, much like I described above. The act of creating can be relaxing, immersed in certain stillness." The experience of creativity cannot be described sufficiently or in ways that is beyond description; it comes and flows through without effort, without the experience of time; minutes may pass, hours may pass and appear like an instant. Creativity does not always happen like this for me. It may seem like a struggle and endless but what I feel is true creativity is effortless and timeless."

To be honest, I do experience both S12's and S13's description of "losing oneself in the process of creating." I lose myself and think of nothing, particularly if I am creating abstract paintings or composing New Age music on my piano computer; but I also experience the creative process driven by my sufferings and creative anguish, where I attempt to get free from my inner self and use the sufferings of the past to create art in more involved works, where I think before I go to create. These differences may have to do with the fact that I am multi-talented and involved in the creative process on a daily basis, perhaps more so than other creative individuals.

My art seems to be deeply concerned with nature and the human condition, much as Picasso has described it in his quote. Perhaps there are still elements of Traumatic Anguish in my creative processes that have become inseparable because I use my creativity as a kind of therapy to let my sad emotions out. And it may well be because of this that the Creative Anguish helps me to cope with my Traumatic Anguish. Art as therapy is not a new concept; there is a body of research that supports the idea that art can function as a therapeutic conduit. Music therapist Juliette Alvin (1966) writes:

"We have three different versions of how the creative process takes place, so who is right and who is wrong? Is creativity inspired by depression, by hypomania, or does it happen while in a mindful state not attached to moods or emotions? I would argue that the creative process is unique to the individual. Some people can create while mildly depressed, while others may be able to do it when mildly hypomanic; some other people may create only when not experiencing any such moods, and this tells us that there is no one way of engaging in the creative process.

It would seem that creativity is not dependent on how a person feels, her or his moods, or other life situation. The creative process is as chaotic and erratic as a storm; it comes and goes. There are no set rules for the creative process and how or why it occurs. Indeed linking it with mental illness serves to support the idea that the creative process is chaotic. People can create while mildly depressed or hypomanic as well as when they are in a mindful state where they lose themselves in their work. I have created my music under all of these circumstances while depressed, hypomanic, and in a state of mindfulness. Creativity was there at all times."

I look forward to the ideas that often emerge from my depression and which I am able to engrave in my artwork, be it painting or poetry or music. I know that my depression is, for me, a source of inspiration. I never had an affliction which did not turn into a painting, or a poem or a song. One of my latest poems was written at the end of one of my deepest depressions:

Mindfulness

We only have moments in which to live.
The future is a concept,
the past is also a concept.
I choose to tune my mind
so that I can play the symphony of life
in perfect harmony.
I know how to fall asleep...
I am learning how to fall awake...

The painting below, titled *Morning Mist*, was also inspired by a period of long and deep depression:

Morning Mist

This poem was also inspired by a deep depression and written right at the end of one of my most severe periods of depression:

The Forgotten People
Written by the Light of the Pale Moon.

The forgotten people
with nowhere to hide,
dreamers of dreams
on whom the pale moon shimmers.

They transform the world,
being one with dreams,
one with love,
one with art.
Ages come and ages go;
this the forgotten people know:
each age has a dream dying,
one that is rising to birth.

Sitting and watching
each age with its dream,
one passing, one emerging
as the pale moon shimmers.

It is impossible to accurately describe the creative process and the situations in which it occurs. The creative process is as different and chaotic as quantum theory, which should perhaps indicate to us that we are looking at the problem from the wrong perspectives. We tend to attribute the creative process to brain functions. But what if the brain has little to do in the actual creative process and it is the heart that has more to do with this mysterious human drive that we know as creativity?

The creative process seems to be chaotic and complex. Creative people may engage in creativity under different circumstances and for different reasons. For some, depression will stimulate creativity and become an expression of the suffering. It may be helpful to remember that extrapolating from personal experience and generalizing it is a dangerous and completely unproductive process.

Discussion and Conclusion

Universities are constantly developing intellectually, but lack in emotional intelligence. This is a concept that was well argued by Kazimierz Dabrowski, who believed that intellectual intelligence without equal development of spiritual/emotional intelligence gives rise to people like Stalin or Hitler, who were very intelligent and, some would say, creative in many ways, but lacked in spiritual development.

As an example of this, we can look at the case of Harvard-educated Berkeley Professor Theodore Kaczynski, also known as the Unabomber, who killed people from 1978 until 1995. This Professor was a genius with a very high IQ and yet, he lacked in spiritual development. If we broaden the concept of intelligence to include heart intelligence, compassion, and social concern, then this professor was not intelligent at all. He was just someone who had an intelligent but automatic mind, a kind of computer deprived of feelings and emotions.

Dabrowski, in his theory of positive disintegration, makes it clear that emotional development (heart intelligence) is extremely important and it is the even development of both intellectual and emotional intelligence which gives rise to the higher citizen, or a person who has high moral standards, and who is willing to forgive, to develop a personality which moves away from self-interest and greed and on to the concern for others. I say this without any resentment or animosity toward the establishment: it is true that Universities need to develop spiritually and need to respect emotions, feelings, and subjective expressions. We need people who have cold, intellectual, and calculating minds, which are also able to be emotional and in touch with their hearts.

The creative artist is a complex human being who often entertains conflicting thoughts. She or he may suffer from a mental illness and this is the case for many artists. It is clear that the pressures of the artistic profession are substantial enough to cause much anxiety and sometimes depression. In addition, many artists seem to gravitate toward professions where they do therapy through art and creativity. While their actual profession may be therapeutic, at another level (that of competition and social relations), it may be extremely stressful.

For many celebrities, the difficulties in keeping up and functioning at one's best in a very competitive environment (where one is as good as one's last performance, exhibition, or piece of writing), it is not difficult to understand the tremendous pressures an artist is under.

For many lesser-known artists, there are many other problems, such as the insecurity of a job market that is highly unstable, where one is never sure about what tomorrow will bring, whether or not they will have a job, or if they will have to risk becoming homeless and end up destitute. Such a stressful life is probably linked to some deviance and, in fact, there is a clear link between creativity and deviance.

While I do not have the time to enter into a discussion of deviance and creativity, I suspect that there are many reasons why creative people engage in deviant behavior. Creative people, whether famous or not, are never treated kindly in our society. For famous people, there is always the media which often brings much anxiety and despair to the minds of celebrities engaged in a constant struggle to avoid publicity, to hide and to fear what may happen if they are not careful in disguising their faces. For less well-known artists, there is often a double stigma—that of being different and of having a mental illness.

If there is a link between creativity and deviance, it is as much the fault of society as it is of the single individual. We tend to exclude creative people from all aspects of social participation unless they are fortunate to make it, in which case they have other more serious worries and problems. We just don't treat our creative people well and we tend to make their lives difficult. That is why many take to drugs and alcohol, engage in minor criminal activities or behave erratically and inappropriately. It is very difficult to conform to a society where the rules are often unsuitable for the more sensitive and creative people.

Above all, we lack heart intelligence in our world. If we had developed heart intelligence, we would not have leaders who have the spiritual development of 3- or 4-year-old ill-tempered toddlers engaged in running entire countries with little to offer toward a better, more just, future.

The highly creative artist is a paradoxical person who has great concern for humanity and yet, on the other hand, is capable of deviance such as using drugs, consuming alcohol, and all the unwanted behavior seen in many artists. We need to begin to help our creative people, help them to achieve. In so doing, we may help many people with mental illness, given that creativity and mental illness often go together. A way to achieve a better social world is by developing a better heart intelligence. For this to happen, we must shift our thinking and our emphasis from research on the brain alone to research that considers the brain-heart as complex entity capable of both intellectual and emotional/spiritual communication. As things are now, many creative people feel more excluded and misunderstood. And it is the same for people with mental illness. To reduce stigma, it would seem, we need to develop our heart intelligence.

What Creative Sufferers Have to Say

Mauro Lopizzo (in Italian):

> ....in effetti tutto parte dal cuore e dalla mente... io ho suonato con tanti musicisti e mi accorgevo chi si esprimeva musicalmente col cuore e chi si esprimeva solo con la tecnica, questi ultimi erano quelli che suonavano solo per danaro e quindi annullavano il sentimento.In effetti è un discorso molto ampio che difficilmente si può affrontare scrivendo.
>
> allora consiglio di leggere un libro di Cristina Nuñez *Someone to Love* una narrazione condotta sul filo dell'emotività che tocca molti momenti della vita personale dell'artista, e poi quello che l'autrice chiama la sua "missione", cioè la divulgazione del metodo "The Self-Portrait Experience" per trasformare la sofferenza umana in arte.

[Translation]

> I feel that both the brain and the heart are involved in the creative process. An artist who expresses her or himself without emotions and feelings is a mechanical artist who has little to offer, apart from technical mastery. But I feel that there is more than just emotions and feelings. Sometimes there is intuition and premonition in art, especially performing arts. Christina Nuñez wrote a book titled *Someone to Love* wherein she writes about converting suffering into art.

Dr Charlotte wrote :

> Alfredo, when I practiced acupuncture, I would treat insomnia and depression very similarly. The heart channel on the body goes up the inside of the arm from the tip of the little finger to the axillary fold. H7, at the wrist, was an important point to needle and so was P6, on the pericardium channel, right next to the heart channel or meridian. The pericardium channel goes up the inside of the arm from the tip of the middle finger to the chest. Studies have shown that acupuncture is very good for pain syndromes and is at least as effective as antidepressants. There are 8 extra channels in addition to the 12 primary ones, and the DU channel is very important for treatment of mental illness. But, like western medicine, a correct diagnosis using pulse technique or evaluation of the tongue along with a

symptom history is essential. I used needling and moxa cones. I, personally, had great success using acupuncture for my patients.

Angela Barbara De Palma wrote:

> For me, "to be an Artist" is more than anything a condition of the Spirit. I have a conception of the Artist. I find that in any human being, this condition can develop: because to be Artists, it means to enter in empathy with the world, being able to understand things from novel perspectives, trying to always put yourself in the clothes of this person or that one, because in reality, the Artist has the ability to see things, the life, the world, through a thousand eyes! The Artist is often able to capture the truth... and to give back it to the world under other forms: it is important to watch the things from various angles (or shots), to always color them with new lights...The Artist must never stop to study, learn, understand, and search: it must be "a continuous search", within and outside of her/himself!

Rose writes:

> Dear Alfredo,
> This is very interesting. Is the person predisposed [DNA-wise] to being extra sensitive and therefore 'artistic in temperament' and tuned into the surroundings, noise, moods, and what's happening in the home [more than siblings] because of the genetically inherited personality traits? For instance, the Depressive person has a thinner lining of the brain. Is that because of the personality type, the chemicals or the DNA type?
> I personally believe that I was born sensitive but that this could have been used to greater artistic value, had my childhood given me a better self esteem.
> I agree with what you've written. I believe that the pain and angst cause us to go and seek an outlet, via acting, singing, painting, playing, music etc.

Salvatore Vinciguerra (in Italian):

> Per quanto riguarda lo stress, devo dirti che quando svolgevo in maniera continuativa l'attività di cantante lo stress era di duplice natura: quello di tipo fiico, per gli spostamenti frequenti, anche di lunga distanza, e andare a letto tardi,e quello psichico del contatto col pubblico: il timore del giudizio per quello che fai, o disbagliare qualcosa in quello che fai.

Un'altra forma di stress era quella con gli editori e i discografici, per la fatica di ottenere l'attenzione e riuscire a oltrepassare il muro degli interessi precostituiti e dei preconcetti. Ovviamente, ogni relazione con gli altri è soggetta a stress, e ritengo che una certa dose sia ineliminabile ed accettabile, fino a che si rivela come stimolo utile e positivo, e riusciamo a recuperare uno stato di serenità oltre tale limite, è meglio evitare—si tratta, per ognuno, di capire in tempo e gestire questo limite mi rendo conto della semplicità e genericità della risposta, nei confronti di una tematica sicuramente più complessa - spero, comunque, che ti serva a qualcosa

[Translation]

Salvatore had lots of problems when he was a performing artist or pop singer. The stress related to his career was so marked that he developed anxiety, depression, and panic attacks. When he changed professions and became a teacher, he felt better and the depression and anxiety went away.

Poppy writes:

"Well, as a child, I always felt different; I wasn't allowed out to play; my guardians [grandparents] were elderly and over-protective in some ways. So I spent my childhood dreaming and drawing and coloring and painting, winning competitions for art, by which I was able to somehow work through the lonely hours that I should have spent in the sun, playing with kids my own age. I also made up stories about the pictures; I invented people in my head, wrote songs, plays, made paper dolls, and made clothes.

I was always aware of texture, the differences in texture in nature, the feel of silk, satin, soft sensuous fabric. I got great joy from changing light patterns in the sky, sunsets. As a child, I found great beauty in nature and liked to be alone with the same. I guess that I began to feel isolated in my world whilst a child at school, timid and preferring my own company to rough company of others. From an early age at school, I felt that I took in a lot of external stimuli, as in people, their moods, the clouds outside, the mood of the teacher, what she was teaching, the colors of the trees on the way home; I always felt there was a glass pane between me and others and never quite broke thru that glass and was bullied.

Moving on to adolescence, I still had a sense of being different. I didn't feel bad about being different; I just questioned everything and found a great outlet of relief through my writing, acting, writing plays, singing, and my art. From growing flowers to setting the table, all had to look well; life to me is art, just a masterpiece with an old ceramic milk jug [French] with natural flowers from the garden. It is a piece of art and I won't let anyone put anything else there. Observing, feeling others' pain, wanting to know more,

I feel that I am very sensitive, that I am prone to depression because of the state of the world; I am deeply upset by what we are doing to the rainforests. I become psychologically very distressed at abuse to animals or elderly or children. I feel things intensely. I know I do because people have remarked on it. I would agree that my personality at times is dramatic, not just to be noticed, but because I perceive people, what they do and say, life in general on a very raw, base level; and I feel it very deeply, living form the heart as I do, so the upside is that I have great and loving friendships, but also that I become very disheartened and hurt and blame myself."

Judy wrote:

To me, being an artist means attempting to give expression in some creative way to how I feel about the world and myself in a way that not only gives others an insight into who I am and my values, but makes them concrete to me and encourages others to examine who they are. The creative result lets me share something that cannot be seen otherwise. I hope that makes sense!

Luigi wrote:

Fresh eyes see different perspectives and originality does not come from rational intellect alone but the whole person. It is the same with art; the skill does not make the work; it is the whole person that is unique and compliments the skill in what becomes a work of art. Every work of art or theory is original, though most often built upon past techniques or knowledge. Being an artist entails a skill and manipulation of that skill through personality, experience, and emotion—all that comprises the unique individual in a work and is a reflection of themselves in the moments of creation and upon their totality as an individual.

16 Heart Intelligence and the Creative Process

When I am depressed, I feel a pain in my heart. I can feel that the beating of the heart is different. My breathing also changes. It is my heart that senses the coming of the depression before the brain. It is like a very strange anxiety, not anxiety proper. In fact, in my journey into mindfulness, I have come to understand that my heart thinks, just like my brain does; in fact, it thinks in a more developed way. I can sense that in my attempt to control my mental sufferings, I must focus on the combination of heart, lungs, and brain as a unit, not as separate organs.

My rational brain tells me that these ideas are unfounded and that I need more proof before I can say/write such wild ideas, but my heart tells me that it is psychic and that it can sometimes sense the future. It can often sense people's intentions, and it can sense dangers in the surrounding environment. When I create artwork or compose music, my heart is at work and I can feel it thinking together with the brain. Following these seemingly strange ideas, I began to do some research on new discoveries about the functioning of the heart. For years, I had been telling people that depression affects the heart more than the brain. To be precise, every organ of the body and every inch of my being are affected by my mental illness. From the top of my head to the bottom of my feet, depression or hypomania affects all of my body. Even later in life, as a university student, I continued to promote this idea and found much rejection amongst academics and mental health experts.

How plausible are these beliefs? Fortunately, new scientific discoveries tend to support my wild ideas very well. There are now cardiologists, professors of neuroscience, and psychiatrists who are aware that there is something magical about the heart.

Professor Mohamed Omar Salem (2007) explains in his essay, "The Heart, Mind and Spirit", that in the future, the heart will be considered an important organ, which affects moods and personality, just as much as the brain in our head.

The information here presented is taken partly from some websites, partly from watching documentaries and partly from the many email communications between myself and various professionals, artists, and scientists from all over the world.

The heart is a thinking, feeling, and sensual organ. It has a very developed memory system, given that it has to remember thousands of functions that it performed in the donor's body, and which, when transplanted, will continue to perform in the new body. If this is true, the following question comes to mind: have we been thinking without a heart? If we feel that the answer may be a "yes", then we'd better wake up and start thinking with our hearts.

There is no doubt at all today that the heart has an inbuilt brain. Images of the heart confirm this. The Intrinsic Cardiac Ganglion has been imaged with startling results: it looks just like brain tissue.

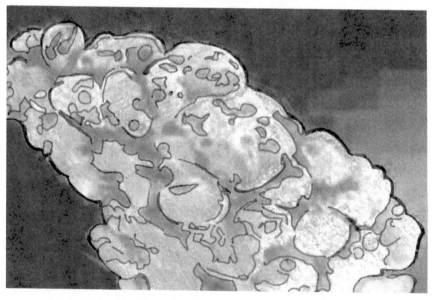

Intrinsic Cardiac Ganglion seen through confocal microscope
Artistic interpretation by Alfredo Zotti

The Intrinsic Cardiac Ganglia are made up of groups of nerve cells (somata) that exist outside of the brain and spinal cord. Each of the smaller circular structures shown is the cell body of an individual neuron.

Surgeons and scientists know today that when the heart is taken out of the body of a donor, it can live up to sixteen hours if cooled to an adequate temperature. When the heart is placed in the recipient's body, all the veins attached, and the heart is profuse with the blood of the recipient, the heart starts to beat spontaneously.

What makes this possible is the little brain in the heart or the Intrinsic Cardiac Ganglion. Consider that the heart has to remember the numerous and complex functions that it was performing hours before, when still in the donor's body. Given that the tasks performed by the heart would take a large room full of machines to be performed, this is in itself undisputable evidence of the thinking capabilities of our heart.

The heart is part of our body that reflects our feelings most accurately. There are numerous different messages that are strongly correlated to our emotional states. The heart sends more information to the brain than the brain does to the heart. It is important to understand the relationship between the heart and the brain because, ultimately, this can tell us how the heart retains memory.

The brain and the heart are in constant communication with each other. These two organs are interconnected by multiple sources, some of which are the neural connections, the hormonal system, pressure receptors, and the actual blood going back and forth to the brain, sending electromagnetic signals. The EKG of the heart is much greater than the EEG of the brain. The heart is the largest generator of electromagnetic fields in the body. The technology today reveals that the magnetic field emitted by the heart can be detected from six feet away. In the future, when machines become more sophisticated, this distance will no doubt increase by many times.

Neurons in the heart are wired together in such a way that they are similar—and in some cases, equal to—the neurons in the brain. Such neurons have short- and long-term memories and the same techniques used to measure brain activity have been used to measure the activity of the Intrinsic Cardiac Ganglion.

If the Intrinsic Cardiac Ganglion can perform similar functions to the brain, then we may ask ourselves: "Can higher memory be stored in the heart and can such memories be transferred with the heart through transplant?" Looking at cases of heart transplant recipients, scientists found that 10% of heart recipients have undergone profound personality changes. The only explanation for such personality changes seems to be that the recipients not only received the heart from the donor, but also some of the memories that were part of the donor's personality and neural system. This is a wild idea, but a professor (S16), in a Spanish email conversation that I have translated here, wrote:

Whenever someone comes up with a wild idea, such an idea needs to be refuted. If it cannot be refuted, then maybe there is something there. We have evidence that some heart transplant recipients receive memories that were part of the donor's personality. We cannot refute this because there is too much evidence.

Dr. Jack Copeland speaks about his latest heart transplant where the patient, Bill, had been transformed into an athlete. After the transplant, the patient found that he was battling with a new transformation and that he was driven by a completely new personality that he had inherited from his donor. He felt as if there were two people living inside of his body. He felt the need to be active and he was now cycling, mountain climbing, running, and doing other various sport activities.

The logical explanation for this was that when we put a new heart in a recipient, we could reproduce some of the memories of the donor's own neural system. It is a plausible explanation. And certainly, the fact that Bill's donor, Michael, was a stunt man who loved all sorts of sports activities seems to support this view. Michael's brother met with Bill because he was curious to meet the person who was now carrying his brother's heart. There was no doubt now that Michael was a true athlete.

Dr Copeland says:

> Bill's idea that he acquired some of his donor's personality since his heart transplant is his idea and I respect it. I cannot say that he is crazy or definitely wrong but, on the other hand, I cannot accept this as a valid interpretation of what is going on without further proof. Nevertheless, I cannot reject the evidence at hand that donors go through a personality change. The idea that the information that exists within a human being can be transferred to another human being through a solid organ is plausible. A powerful organ such as the heart could certainly generate personality change once placed in a new neural system situation (BBC Channel 4 TV, 2006).

Is there further evidence for these claims? Professor Bruce Hood, University of Bristol, was interviewed by the BBC News:

> Some of the psychological changes many patients experience have very good physiological explanations; however, according to one survey of transplant patients, approximately one in three attributes this change to taking on psychological characteristics of the donor even though conventional science has generally rejected the idea that such transference is possible (BBC 2009).

> However strange these ideas are, research has found one in three organ transplant patients believes they have taken on some aspects of the donor's personality... Essentially, they believe they will somehow take on those characteristics of the donor ...(ibid)

The implications of these discoveries are certainly profound. What this information demonstrates is that our current science is ill-equipped to deal with mystic phenomena. Our science works well for quantifiable research, but it is unable to explain or study mystical experiences. We have not yet begun to consider just how this will change our perception of memory, thinking, and even the meaning of life. If the heart is truly intelligent, then we certainly have forgotten how to think with our hearts. For artists, philosophers, and scientists, this new knowledge will inspire new research and new ways of understanding human nature. The fact that we are social beings seems to be closely related to the concept of heart intelligence.

There have already been some changes in the scientific community. For example, starting with the assumption that the heart is intelligent, some experiments have been carried out.

The heart is intuitive. The heart responds to disturbing photos before these appear on the screen and sends the message to the brain milliseconds before the picture is perceived. The information travels to the brain that prepares the body for possible action and response to the negative picture. Usually, expressions of sorrow or pain are captured by the camera. Rollin McCarty, of the Institute of HeartMath, has conducted important research in an attempt to investigate the intuitive heart hypothesis. He writes:

> **Design:** The study used a counterbalanced crossover design, in which 30 calm and 15 emotionally arousing pictures were presented to 26 participants under two experimental conditions: a baseline condition of normal psychophysiologic function and a condition of physiological coherence. Primary measures included: skin conductance, the electroencephalogram (EEG), from which cortical event-related potentials and heartbeat-evoked potentials were derived, and the electrocardiogram (ECG), from which cardiac decelerations/accelerations were derived. These measures were used to investigate where and when in the brain and body intuitive information is processed.
>
> **Results:** The study's results are presented in two parts. The main findings in relation to the heart's role in intuitive perception presented here are: (1) surprisingly, the heart appears to receive and respond to intuitive information; (2) a significantly greater heart rate deceleration occurred prior to future emotional stimuli compared to calm stimuli; (3) there were

significant gender differences in the processing of prestimulus information. Part 2 will present results indicating where in the brain intuitive information is processed and data showing that prestimulus information from the heart is communicated to the brain. It also presents evidence that females are more attuned to intuitive information from the heart.

Conclusions: Overall, we have independently replicated and extended previous research documenting prestimulus responses. It appears that the heart is involved in the processing and decoding of intuitive information. Once the prestimulus information is received in the psychophysiologic systems, it appears to be processed in the same way as conventional sensory input. This study presents compelling evidence that the body's perceptual apparatus is continuously scanning the future. To account for the results presented in Parts 1 and 2, Part 3 will develop a theory based on holographic principles explaining how intuitive perception accesses a field of energy into which information about future events is spectrally enfolded (McCarty, Atkinson, and Bradley 2004).

This means two things: The heart is connected to an external field of knowledge, and the heart is intuitive and psychic.

I looked for information on whether or not others have done the same experiment. I know from experience that I often use my heart to think before I use my brain. This is particularly so whenever I start an artwork. I often need to feel emotions and I need to feel that anguish in my heart before my first brush stroke. There are scientific experiments that confirm what I am saying here.

The heart has been proven to be intuitive and to be connected to an external field of knowledge. This would explain psychic phenomena or telepathy. Also—and here is the disturbing (amazing?) idea—we are all potentially capable of being psychic or telepathic. It is just that we have forgotten how to use our heart and mind in combination because of our corporate world that has conditioned us to live more like machines than people. In the future, the heart will be considered to be a thinking organ which has a specific function within the limbic system. Mental illness will be approached with the notion that the heart, lungs, and brain work and think in combination. The heart has its own particular intelligence which is unique and we, as evidence shows, have forgotten how to use it. What are the implications of all of this for our management and understanding of mental anguish, be it labeled Schizophrenia, Anxiety, PTSD, OCD, Bipolar or Depression?

Before I answer this question, please listen to what a doctor (S15) who used Chinese medicine told me in an email exchange:

> "Alfredo, when I practiced acupuncture I would treat insomnia and depression very similarly. The heart channel on the body goes up the inside of the arm from the top of the little finger to the auxiliary fold. H7, at the wrist, was an important point to needle and so was P6, on the pericardium channel, right next to the heart channel or meridian. The pericardium channel goes up the inside of the arm from the tip of the middle finger to the chest. Studies have shown that acupuncture is very good for pain syndrome and is at least as effective as antidepressants. There are 8 extra channels in addition to the 12 primary ones, and the DU channel is very important for treatment of mental illness. But, like western medicine, a correct diagnosis using pulse technique or evaluation of the tongue along with symptom history is essential. I used needling and moxa cones. I, personally, had great success using acupuncture for my patients".

This is interesting because, as professor Salem (2004) argues:

> In many cultures throughout history, the heart has been considered the source of emotions, passion, and wisdom. Also, people used to feel that they experienced the feeling or sensation of love and other emotional states in the area of the heart. However, in the past, scientists emphasized the role of the brain in the head as being responsible for such experiences. Interestingly, recent studies have explored physiological mechanisms by which the heart communicates with the brain, thereby influencing information processing, perceptions, emotions, and health. These studies provided the scientific basis to explain how and why the heart affects mental clarity, creativity, and emotional balance.

It is difficult to dismiss the latest research on the heart. Some scientists may argue that the heart has only 40,000 neuron cells and that this, compared to the billions of neuron cells in the brain, is not enough to define the heart as an organ that is intelligent in its own right. It is not clear if neurons need to be in the millions to work effectively, nor if the neurons in the heart are exactly the same as those in the brain. We have no definite proof of anything. Yet, we cannot dismiss research on cellular memory, nor the fact that some heart transplant recipients inherit the personalities of their donors.

In addition, research on premonition and intuition of the heart cannot be ruled out, particularly after repeated experiments such as the photographs experiment that I have discussed in this journal. It is clear that something is going on and that we need to do more research on heart intelligence. Currently, we are spending a lot of money on brain research (fMRI brain scans) and not enough on brain and heart interaction. We cannot dismiss heart intelligence as nonsense. Unfortunately, this is what many academics are doing with some arrogance and ignorance. William James once wrote, "If you want to disprove the law that all crows are black, it is enough if you prove one single crow to be white" (Bellecci 2002).

For an artist like me, heart intelligent may just be the missing link that can explain the creative process in terms of premonition, intuition and being in touch with an external source of energy/knowledge, perhaps consciousness itself. As intelligent and valued members of society, we need to support research on heart intelligence and the brain-heart interaction, not only for our present benefit, but for future generations.

Next time we hear or read that an artist like Tom Yorke, the lead singer of *Radiohead*, saying that his ideas get "beamed" at him from a place of which little is known, it may well be that his heart is in tune with an external source of knowledge; or, similarly, when mathematician Ramanujan says that he was given the miraculous answer to a mathematical dilemma by the gods, perhaps he also means that somehow he was in touch with an external field of knowledge. We may remain skeptical about this, but given that we are so very ignorant about many mysteries of the universe, we would be best to remain humble and just say that we don't know what is happening and that artists or great mathematicians are not stupid. It is clearly that something out of the ordinary is often going on in the creative process about which we know nothing.

17 Disability— Don't Dismiss My Ability

The creative process is very complex to describe and I feel that I need to write more about it here. I include an essay which sheds some light on the creativity of the famous French painter Henri de Toulouse-Lautrec (1864 - 1901). I hope this can better help us to understand the internal conflicts and physical or mental illnesses that often fuel the creative process.

Toulouse was a disabled man who had tremendous artistic talents and empathy for less fortunate people. He was never at ease with his disability and he became bitter about life, drowning his sorrows in, and coping with physical pain using alcohol. Those who judged him by his looks, given that he was deformed, believed he was a drunken, vice-ridden court jester whose friends were pimps and girls from brothels; for those who wanted to know more about Toulouse, they found a highly intellectual and caring young man who found spiritual refuge and acceptance amongst the poorer people, the artists, and those who lived the nightlife. The less fortunate people, the working people, are often willing to overlook disabilities and human faults and take the person as they are, something that, in my experience, is less often the case, usually, amongst middle and upper classes. Whichever way we look at it, Toulouse Lautrec is today remembered as one of the greatest visual artists who ever lived.

Lautrec was born Henri Marie Raymond de Toulouse-Lautrec-Monfa on 24 November 1864, in Albi, Tarn, France. He was the first-born of Comte Alphonse and Comtesse Adele de Toulouse-Lautrec. His brother was born on 28 August 1867, but died the following year. Although he is today known as Toulouse Lautrec, his first name was Henri.

Henri suffered with a number of congenital defects, attributed to inbreeding. The Napoleonic abolition of primogeniture had prompted an already much-reduced French nobility to keep what wealth remained in their families by the simple expedient of not marrying out of their family.

Henri de Toulouse-Lautrec
Drawing by Alfredo Zotti

His mother and father were first cousins. At the age of 13, Henri fractured his left leg and the next year, he fractured the right one. Today's physicians attribute this to an unknown genetic disorder sometimes named "Toulouse Lautrec Syndrome." The disorder is along the lines of osteopetrosis (which means "stone-bone", and not to be confused with osteoporosis) or anchondroplasia. As a consequence of the injuries, his legs ceased to grow and he looked much like a dwarf, with the exception that his torso was fully grown while his legs were abnormally short. He was 4 feet, 11 inches tall. He also had hypertrophied genitals.

Because of his disabilities, he was unable to participate in normal activities, particularly sports, and for this reason, he devoted himself to his art, immersing himself in the work. He became a world-renowned painter, printmaker, illustrator (*Le Rire* magazine 1890) and draftsman whose work portrayed the theatrical and decadent images of modern life in 19th century France.

Lautrec was an extremely intelligent man whose major problem was that he developed sarcasm and cynicism simply because he could not accept his disabilities. Many critics have argued that it was a sort of physical self-loathing that caused him to seek and portray all that was most vicious and harsh of Paris. But Paris of the 19th century could be a very vicious and harsh place. On one occasion, looking at one of the many portraits he had done of her, Yvette Guilbert remarked, "Really, Lautrec, you are a genius of deformity." He replied, "Why, of course I am." Stigma and prejudice have a double edge, for while some people are quick to discriminate and point to one's misfortunes, looking down on the disabled, nothing is worse than one who is not able to live with one's own defects. Henri became an alcoholic and a womanizer, just like his father, who had little time for Henri and his mother. His mother, on the other hand, was a religious woman who loved and tolerated him, understanding that he was a true artist. Henri remained resentful and dependent on his mother throughout his short life. He died in his mother's arms at the age of 37, due to alcoholism and syphilis, after a short stay at a Parisian sanitarium where he was put because of having developed mental problems due to these diseases. He continued to paint to show the doctors there that he was recovering and back to his normal self. This inability to cope was what drove Henri Toulouse Lautrec to drink himself to death, committing a slow suicide. He was aware that he was killing himself.

Lautrec was interested in the psychology of classes other than his own. He studied people and became obsessed with women who were to play such a vital part in his life. Lautrec respected and enjoyed the company of women (even prostitutes) and he also liked animals, particularly horses, but he did not feel the same toward men, seeing most of them as destructive. He came to believe that women were spontaneous and more in tune with nature, while men were the opposite. The few men whom he tolerated, and found interesting, were other artists and especially writers like Oscar Wilde, who had become a good friend. He was particularly fond of van Gogh and, indeed, van Gogh and Lautrec had studied together in Cormon's atelier and the two had become friends. Vincent once invited Lautrec to be part of an exhibition of new artists in a working-class restaurant of Paris in 1887. Vincent's brother, Theo, became Lautrec's art dealer and the three lunched together in Paris just three weeks before Vincent van Gogh fatally shot himself in 1890.

I do see some similar techniques in Lautrec and van Gogh paintings. Lautrec, unlike van Gogh, had been able to establish himself as an artist and, in 1888, his work began to sell well. His posters were so popular, in fact, that some people were known to follow the workmen who glued them to the walls, so that they could peel them off before the glue dried. The newspaper of the time, *La Vie Parisienne*, wrote: "You can't go any-where without finding yourself face-to-face with Aristide Bruant." Aristide Bruant was a singer who performed at the Moulin Rouge and Lautrec made a portrait of the singer, and consequently, many posters were made that were distributed all over France.

During his career, Henri created 737 canvases, 275 watercolors, 363 prints, over 5000 drawings and many other works, some of which have been lost. Today, he is known as one of the great post-impressionist painters along with van Gogh, Gauguin, and Cezanne; but more than this, he was exceptionally original.

By the late 1890s, Lautrec had exhibited his work all over Europe, in England and the United States. He created a new genre, but also added new techniques to the art of lithography. Thanks to Lautrec, two major events took place: the birth of modern printmaking and the explosion of the night life culture. The French economy benefited tremendously in terms of tourism, which generated jobs. All this was possible because of the efforts of one physically disabled and creative young man. Hence, we should never dismiss anyone's abilities and this is a lesson important for people and important for governments, industries, and all social organiza-tions, which still tend to exclude some disabled people who could contribute tremendously to society.

Montmartre and Moulin Rouge

Montmartre is a 130-meter high hill, north of Paris, in the 18th arrondissement (district), a part of the Right Bank, which gives the name to the surrounding district of Montmartre[8]. The district of Montmartre was notorious for its brothels and thieves and also because of its hangouts for avant-garde artists like Cezanne, van Gogh, and Picasso. It was a world were intellectuals, artists, thieves, prostitutes, and people from all walks of life coexisted. This was where "real life" was to be found, something that for an artist like Lautrec was irresistible.

The Moulin Rouge was a cabaret and night club built in 1889 by Joseph Oller, who also owned the Paris Olympia. It is set on the affluent edge of Montmartre, in the Paris district of Pigalle, on Boulevard de Clichy, because to venture into the centre of the district was dangerous and for this reason, it was built in this ideal place. When the Moulin Rouge dance hall opened its doors, one of Henri's circus paintings adorned the entrance hall.

Henri spent much time in night clubs and brothels, particularly the Moulin Rouge, where he found his most interesting subject to portray. Toulouse's posters made Moulin Rouge infamous throughout Europe and people often traveled from afar to visit.

It is at the Moulin Rouge that a modern form of the ancient can-can dance was born, which evolved into a form of entertainment of its own and led to the introduction of cabarets across Europe. One of the most famous dancers, whom Lautrec portrayed on numerous occasions in his posters, was a strawberry-blond named Louise Weber, better known as "La Goulue" (The Glutton). A former prostitute, she became popular for dancing the *chahut* (slang for chaos), an erotic form of the can-can, and was noted for kicking the top hats off men's heads as she danced. Some described her as a strange girl with a tortured mouth and metallic eyes.

The Moulin Rouge is a tourist destination for visitors from around the world who like musical dance entertainment or are interested in the history and like to walk in the same streets or be in the same buildings where some of the great artists of our times spent much of their time. Some of the romance of the turn-of-the-century France is still present in the club's decor.

In the early years of the Moulin Rouge, extravagant shows, inspired by the circus and attractions that are still famous, such as Pétomane, were common occurrences. Concert dances are still organized every day at 10 pm.

On 22 June 1951, Georges France, who was called Jo France, founder of the Balajo, acquired the Moulin Rouge and renovated it. He gave Henri Mahé, one of the most fashionable architects of the day, the task of improving and fitting out the new auditorium. The décor envisaged by Jo

---

[8] http://en.wikipedia.org/wiki/Montmartre

France and largely realized by Henri Mahé still delights contemporary visitors.[9]

Many movies and documentaries have been made about Moulin Rouge and the last film (2001) was directed by Baz Luhrmann with actors Nicole Kidman and Ewan McGregor. John Leguizamo played the part of Toulouse Lautrec. This was a movie that picked up six Golden Globe Award nominations. It received 13 nominations at the BAFTA awards. The film received eight Oscar nominations, including best actress in a leading role for Nicole Kidman. The movie was shot in Sydney. It was a very successful movie grossing, worldwide, nearly $180 million.

It is true to say that there is something magical about Moulin Rouge, not only because of the entertainment and the nightlife, but also because of the history and the fact that many great artists were part of that life and visited the Moulin Rouge, which became a sort of Mecca for great artists and intellectuals.

Turn-of-the Century France and Lautrec's posters

At the time when Lautrec was following, and even stalking, his subjects around the nightclubs and brothels of Paris in order to study and draw them, French anarchism could turn very violent in a moment. A bomb was tossed and exploded in the legislature in 1893 and the French president, Sadi Carnot, was assassinated the following year. In Montmartre, however, acts of terror were translated into radical art; that was the way in which the people of Montmartre fought against the system. Lautrec was someone who disliked the system, for he could see a multitude of problems in the way that many people were marginalized. And it is in the marginal people of society that he found comfort, understanding and acceptance of his disabilities. Moreover, he felt that the marginal people were most natural and spontaneous and this was ideal for his portraits, for he wanted to portray real life and real people who had genuine existential concerns. For these reasons, he became friends with prostitutes, pimps, radical artists, and particularly writers who, at the time, desired change for the better.

Lautrec had respect for the prostitutes, whom he probably saw as women who had been able to succeed in beating the system and able to create a life for themselves, however troubled and unpleasant, in order to survive. In many of his posters, he portrayed prostitutes with dignity and even gave them tender and delicate expressions. The prostitutes were his models and in his presence, they were just women and he treated them as equals.

[9] http://en.wikipedia.org/wiki/Moulin_rouge

Henri's art was unique. It was influenced by Japanese art of the time, especially the Japanese Ukiyo-e prints. Large areas of pure and flat color, strong outlines, cropped compositions and silhouettes, along with oblique angles, were typical of the work of Japanese artists like Ando Hiroshige (1858) and Katsushika Hokusai (1849). And, just as in the Edo–period Japan performers and famous actors were portrayed in woodblock prints, so, too, Lautrec used the posters to portray the entertainers of the time and, in doing so, combined art with the business side of things. His posters became not only beautiful artworks, but were useful in advertising and promoting the nightlife of Paris, both locally and internationally. Unlike Van Gogh, Lautrec made a lot of money from the sale of his posters, which he spent on drinks and women, possibly because he was not that concerned with material possessions or the accumulation of wealth. His main interest was his art.

Lautrec's art is unique in that it seeks to capture the spontaneous expressions of the people of Paris. Lautrec had a photographic memory and his paintings reveal an incredible technique that captures the expression of the sitter. His paintings are more like photographs that are able to freeze time and capture that wonderful expression, that wonderful moment that will not come back but has been frozen and immortalized in a still life. Lautrec was also concerned with movement and, indeed, he was fascinated with horses, which were featured in many of his paintings.

His oil paintings were preparations for his posters, evidence that for Lautrec, commercial art was not inferior to real art, just an extension of it. Indeed, there is reason to believe that Lautrec preferred his posters to his oil paintings, essentially because the posters were simpler, with fewer elements, and yet, because of this, even more powerful than oil paintings. The simplicity of his work and "what was missing" was what made his art so wonderful and unique.

There is no doubt that he had a tremendous influence on both artists of his time and later artists like Picasso and Andy Warhol. He was a deformed man with a normal torso and undeveloped legs, with a pendulous bottom lip and without real teeth, who drooled frequently and was constantly drunk. He consumed large amounts of alcohol to cope with pain, as well, given that the bones of his legs were so painful. Yet behind all of his disabilities, behind his deformity and drunkenness, there was a genius who studied life and attempted to capture human frailties, the wonderful expressions of sorrow, fear, lust, innocence, and all that is spontaneous of humans. Spontaneity and honesty he found in the marginal people of society, people who had no pretences and understood the harshness of life. From this perspective, Lautrec could study life and he felt that he belonged to those people; that he was one of them, something he did not feel amongst his aristocratic class.

There is a lesson for all of us here, especially for the middle and upper classes, and that is that we cannot judge a book by its cover. Today, in a world where we tend to exclude many people for a variety of reasons (disabled people, people with mental illness, and even people who are middle-aged and often excluded from the workforce), we need to reconsider our ideology and ponder on the possibility that inside that disabled person, someone with a mental illness, or an older person, there may well be a Toulouse Lautrec waiting to express her or his talents and gifts and in so doing, advance society. We can never dismiss someone's abilities just because of their disability.

Conclusion

Like other mental disorders, Bipolar Disorder is so complex that I feel we do not understand it completely. My particular bipolar disorder II appears to me to be part of my personality. The main feature of this disorder is the depression.

It has not been easy for me to learn to control my depression. And I feel that I developed depression partly by imitating the behavior of my father and mother, who both suffered with depression. What I mean here is that I developed certain responses to life stressors and negative situations, by doing exactly what my parents were doing: despair, become depressed and hopeless, and let other family members help them. On top of it, my father was a serious alcoholic. One day he was unhappy and the next he would be quite happy. He was mostly happy when intoxicated; but as we know, when the effect of alcohol ends, depression sets in because alcohol is a depressant. One day, my father would sing opera and swing the cat by the tail. The world was beautiful and I felt happy, tremendously happy because my father was happy. But sometimes my father was miserable so that I felt immensely sad. That was how my bipolar was shaped: moments of happiness mixed with moments of sadness. The more my father's behavior went on, the more the moods intensified to become a full-scale disorder.

My parents were very intelligent, creative, and good-hearted people; but they were not perfect and their behavior shaped my mental disorder.

A child will imitate the parents' behavior and how they deal with life events. But the Bipolar II was also generated by my sensitive personality. In this way, I see my sensitivity and creativity as genetic components of my depressive personality (not that this can be measured by identifying genetic bipolar codes. To this day, the genetic explanation of mental illness is based on much speculation. We are simply not certain about what is going on.

It took many years of practice for me to be able to learn other responses to life situations and life stressors. What saved me, and it is the same situation for my wife who suffers with bipolar 1, is that we both lived and were raised by our grandparents. While I lived occasionally with my parents, I spent most of my childhood and teenage life with my grandparents because my parents travelled throughout Europe as I stated before. While my father's alcoholism traumatized me since I was four, and later as a teenager when we came to Australia, my childhood days, from six years of age to when I was about eleven, were spent with my grandparents. My wife, on the other hand, was taken away from her stepmother who mistreated her, and given to her grandparents. She lived with them since she was four. What our grandparents taught us was joy for life, empathy for the world, the importance of creativity, and the importance of being a good and moral person. Both my wife and I have this in common and I feel that our grandparents saved us from a terrible life. The grandparents restored some trust in humanity and showed us that life can be beautiful, no matter what.

It was not until my 30s that I really started to live a full and productive life. I was a musician then. What helped me to change was my experience of being homeless, of helping other people like me, of trying to understand life and people. I guess I took an intellectual path, but one filled with information and feedback from real life experience. In fact, one of the reasons why I cannot study at university today is because I know that universities exclude emotions and feelings, essential parts of experience and knowledge.

Anyway, going back to my depression, it is not easy to control it. From one angle, it is important that I let my depression find expression. We do need to become sad, and even cry, when depressed. I usually let emotions out by listening to music and songs with which I can relate, and that are meaningful to how I feel. Sometimes I play and compose music, but this usually happens later when the depression begins to lift.

My depression comes as a tremendous sense of anxiety, a feeling that something terrible is happening and I feel this pain in the chest and the heart. It is an overbearing mixture of heaviness, sad emotions and a sense that the world is about to end. We do need to let this take over a bit, and express itself, whether in a poem or in writing. Writing is wonderfully therapeutic. But at the same time, we cannot let the depression get a hold of us completely and force us to stay in bed. We can struggle to prevent this and this is the difficult part. The Buddhist concept of acceptance helps. What is, is. For now, I am depressed, and I can accept that.

This requires strength and determination, but the good thing is that once one is able to do this, one finds a sense of achievement, self-respect, and strength. One is then able to control the depression, and this is a real milestone. It can be done. For example, any mental illness can be controlled by the mind. Perhaps not fully controlled, and there will always be times when the mental illness takes over. But our mind can learn to keep things under control most of the times. Carl Jung, the famous psychiatrist, suffered with symptoms of schizophrenia and so did the Nobel laureate John Nash. They learned to use their mental disorder, their schizophrenia, to fuel their genius. In fact, the experience of schizophrenia is what helped Jung come up with such an amazing theory of archetypes and spirituality.

When depression comes today, I immediately think about two things: it is not permanent; and some wonderful piece of artwork, music, or writing will come out of it. I am happy about these. That is what helps me. And when you put this kind of intelligence together with the strength that I have developed over the years (it does not mean that I don't get sick sometimes, but it does mean that I cope much better than I would otherwise do and that I am in control more often than not), you can only call this Emotional and Spiritual Intelligence. I have a long way to go, but I am at a good point in this journey, perhaps more than half way there.

In the beginning of my struggle to cope with my moods, I just wanted to vent and share with those who had similar experiences. The internet has made this possible for me. At that time, I just wanted plain and simple support. At this stage in my journey, however, simple support is not the only thing that I need. I also need some truth, though that cannot be fully achieved. I just want to get near the truth. I want to say to the world that I helped myself with my mind. It wasn't the medications; it wasn't therapy; it was nothing like that. It was my mind. Until I decided to help myself, making up my mind, nothing worked for me. Once I decided to help myself with my mind, everything else started to work: the occasional medication that I take a few months of the year started to work for me; the therapy offered by my psychologist started to work for me. Everything started to work. All change comes from within.

But before things could help me, I had to let the mind decide to help itself. I had to take responsibility for my Bipolar II and stop letting others pick up the pieces. I had to pick up the pieces and put them together. I was responsible. The mind can heal itself and it can also watch over itself. Even if we occasionally become unable to be in control, due to our emotional and behavioral disabilities, we still need to persevere and struggle.

If we were just biological machines, this should not be possible from a scientific perspective. Indeed, consciousness is a huge question for hardcore scientists. They are searching for consciousness in the brain; but the thing is that while the brain can perceive consciousness, there is every indication that consciousness may be an energy that exists outside of the human body, the force that animates the universe. If every human on

Earth was to disappear, would the world continue to exist? Most probably yes, and the animals, plants, and insects would continue to feel conscious about being alive. This, after all, was the perspective of the ancient Greeks, the geniuses of their time whose ideas we seem to disregard today. After all, even animals get depressed. This is part of the evidence that they are conscious of their lives.

My mental illness is not an illness at all. It is just the way I am, the way that I have developed because of various environmental forces, such as traumatic experiences. The mental disorder is today an aspect of my personality and has both risks and benefits. And this kind of personality is not an ideal one in our western world, because the kind of journey that I have experienced has turned me into a curious, intelligent human being who questions everything and who is very careful and aware of ideologies and myths. It is a rebellious personality, because it constantly tries to seek and highlight the truth, and we want to keep away from it; we want to sweep it under the rug. And in many ways, I feel that this is what a true artist is, someone who seeks the truth and in doing so alienates many people who are not ready to confront the truth for whatever reason.

That is why we have so many myths and ideologies in our society, because we avoid the truth. The plain truth may be painful, but it is better to know it than to remain ignorant and oblivious to what is going on. The myth of mental illness is one of the powerful, yet destructive myths of our western world. It fuels stigma. I do have a mental disorder and will probably have it for the rest of my life. With social support and care, I can do wonderful things. But I must state with great emphasis that I do not have a mental illness. I have a mental disorder, which for me is more of a blessing than a curse. I accept it and use it to become a better person. And I am fortunate to have found many wonderful people who, like me, suffer in silence and use the suffering to get closer to the Light.

What has really helped me to control my severe moods is the ability to look at the truth, no matter how painful, and to put up with the pain of knowing. I think that deep in our hearts, we do know that only when we decide to help ourselves will any kind of therapies work. In other words, if our mind does not want help, all will fail. And because of this, I claim that the mind can heal itself. I used to leave things to others and fail to become responsible to help myself. While I did this, nothing really helped me.

What is mental illness? A necessary aspect of some human beings that is essential to the progress and advancement of humanity. Yet we want to medicate it away. With it, we will probably medicate genius away, and I hope this does not happen. I feel that depression is part of the human suffering that propels humanity toward greater achievements. In this sense, I feel gifted and special. I don't feel that I am a mistake, or someone who is disabled and ready for the scrap heap. This is what our ignorant society wants us to believe, but this is not how I see things.

I have a mental disorder that arose during my childhood development by numerous traumatic experiences, the fact that I am very sensitive and creative, and the fact that I imitated my parents' behavior. But in no way is my mind sick. On the contrary, my mind is much more lucid than that of many other people. I may not always perform as those who do not suffer with a mental disorder and I will remain affected, by past experiences and genetics, for the rest of my life. But I do contribute, in my way, to the advancement of knowledge and I am a constructive and hardworking human being.

I have presented my story, because I think it is similar in many ways to the stories of others who experience Bipolar. Looking at this case study, you can see where Bipolar comes from, and what has worked for me in constructively living with it. If, like me, you can look on Bipolar as the negative side of the blessing of creativity and uniqueness, if you can experimentally check out which of my coping mechanisms will work for you, then you will put another silver lining on my cloud: the fact that I have been of service to you.

References

Berk, M. & Dodd, S. (2005). Bipolar II disorder: a review. *Bipolar Disorders*, 7, 11-21

Cannetti, Elias (1984). *Crowds and Power* (in English). New York: Farrar, Straus and Giroux.

Darwin, C. (1968/1859). *On the origin of the species*, Harmondsworth: Penguin Books.

Dawkins, R. (1989). *The selfish gene*. Oxford: University Press.

Easton, L. D. & Guddat, K. H. (1969). *Writing of the young Marx on philosophy and society*. United States of America: Anchor Books.

Fisher, E. (1970). *Marx in his own words*. London: Allan Lane/The Penguin Press.

Haralambos, M & Holborn, M. (1995). *Sociology: themes and perspectives*. London: Collins Educational.

Hindess, B. (1987). *Freedom, equality and the market*. Tavistock Publications, London.

Kropotkin, P. A., Huxley, T. H., & Paul Avrich. (1955). *Mutual aid, a factor of evolution*. Boston: Extending Horizons Books.

Leahy, T. (1996). *Sociological utopias and social transformation: permaculture and the gift economy*. Newcastle, Australia: The University of Newcastle.

Mandel, E, & Novack, G. (1979). *The Marxist theory of alienation*. New York: Pathfinder Press.

McLellan, D. (1973). *Karl Marx: his life and thought*. London: McMillian Press

Mitchell, L. (2003, July) Utopia rising. *The Age*. Retrieved from http://www.theage.com.au/articles/2003/07/02/1056825453141.html

Ruse, M. (1986). *Taking Darwin Seriously*, Oxford University Press: New York/ Oxford.

Singer, P. (1993). *How are we to live?* The text publishing company: Australia.

Smith, A. (1723-1797). *An enquiry into the nature and causes of the wealth of nations,* Dublin: Messers Whitestone.

Spencer, H. (1884). *Principles of biology.* London: Williams & Norgate.

Weber, M. (1958). *The protestant ethic and the spirit of capitalism.* New York: Charles Scriber's Sons.

References for Counseling and Clinical Psychology

American, Psychiatric Association, (1980). *Diagnoatic and statistical manual of mental disorders (3d.ed.)* Washington, DC: Author.

APS College competencies specification of areas of specialist knowledge and skills (1997). The Australian psychological society. CAN 000 543 788. Retrieved from http://www.psychology.org.au/Assets/Files/competencies_of_aps_college_members.pdf

Burton, L., Westen, D. & Kowalski, R. (2012). *Psychology: Australian and New Zealand Edition.* (3rd Ed.). Milton, Qld: John Wiley & Sons.

Davidson, G., C. and Neale, M., J. (1990). *Abnormal psychology.* (5th.Ed.). John Wiley & Sons: New York.

Dluzewska, T., clinical psychologist, Psych 1200 lecture notes, 14 of March 2012.

Doidge, N., (2007). The brain that changes itself. *Penguin Books,* London

Grant, J., Mullings, B., Denham, G. (2008). Couselling psychology in Australia: past, present and future—part one. *The Australian journal of counseling psychology.* Retrieved from http://www.groups.psychology.org.au/Assets/Files/Counselling%20Psychology%20in%20Australia%20%282%29.pdf

HCCC website http://www.hccc.nsw.gov.au/

Linfrods, L., and Arden, J., B. (2009). Brain-based therapy and the 'Pax Medica'. *Psychotherapy in Australia.* Vol. 15 NO 3, MAY 2009.

Mason, Martin and Tatterstall, (2011) Conflict of interest: a review of institutional policies in Australian medical schools. *MJA,* Volume 194, number 3, 7 February 2011.

Norcross, J.C., Karg, R., & Prochask, J. O. (1997). Clinical psychologists in the 1990's.II. *The Clinical Psychologist,* 50, 4-11.

Norcross, J. C., Sayette, M. A., Mayne, T. J., Karg, R. S., & Turkson, M. A. (1998). Selecting a doctoral program in professional psychology: Some comparisons among PhD counseling, PhD clinical, and PsyD clinical psychology programs. *Professional Psychology: Research and Practice, 29,* 609-614.

Norcross, J.C. (2012). Clinical vs counseling psychology: what's the diff? *Psi the international honor society in psychology.* Retrieved from: http://www.psichi.org/pubs/articles/article_73.aspx

Psychologist Registration Act. (2000). Report n41 assented the 6th of June 2000. Retrieved from

http://www.legislation.vic.gov.au/Domino/Web_Notes/LDMS/Pub
Statbook.nsf/f932b66241ecf1b7ca256e92000e23be/be4ea1f13e00
f053ca256e5b00213e56/$FILE/00-041a.pdf

Olujie, C., clinical psychologist, Psych 1200 lecture, 28 of March 2012.
PBA website http://www.psychologyboard.gov.au/

Reznic, O. (2006). *The secrets of medical decision making.* Loving
Healing Press: New York.

Rich, B., counseling psychologist, personal communication. 2012.

The Australian Psychological Society (APS) Code of Ethics Retrieved from
http://www.psychology.org.au/Assets/Files/Code_Ethics_2007.pdf

Watkins, C., E. Counseling psychology, clinical psychology, and human
services psychology: Where the twain shall meet? *American
Psychologist*, Vol 40(9), Sep 1985, 1054-1056.

Whitfield, L. (2010). Psychotic Drugs as Agents of Trauma by Charles L.
Whitfield, MD. Excerpted from: *The International Journal of Risk
and Safety in Medicine* 22 (2010) 195-207 DOI 10.3233/JRS-
2010-0508. IOS Press. Volume 22, Number 4, 2010.

Zook, A. On the merger of clinical and counseling psychology.
Professional Psychology: Research and Practice, Vol 18(1), Feb
1987, 4-5.

References for Science and Art of Psychology

Churchland, P, M. (1993). *Matter and consciousness: A contemporary introduction to the philosophy of mind*, MIT Press, Cambridge, Massachusetts, London, England.

Doidge, N., (2007). *The brain that changes itself*. Penguin books, London.

Eisenk, H. The effect of psychotherapy: an evaluation. *Journal of counseling psychology*, 16, 319-324.

Gardner, H (2005). *Scientific Psychology: should we bury it or prise it?* Chapter 5, pp77-90. From Steinberg, J, R. Unity in psychology: possibility or pipedream? American Psychological Association, Washington. D.C.

Griffeath, D, Modelling snow crystal growth I: History, Morphology, and Remaining Riddles, *UW Math Probability Semionar, Spring 2006* retrieved from http://www.math.wisc.edu/~seppalai/old-probsem/probsem-S06.html 14-Nov-2012.

Holmes, J (1993) *Between Art and Science: essays in psychotherapy and psychiatry*, Tavistock/Routledge, London and New York.

Rich, R. Counseling Psychologist, personal email communication, November 2012.

World Health Organization, Constitution of the World Health Organization, retrieved from http://www.who.int/governance/eb/who_constitution_en.pdf on the 14-Nov-2012.

References for CBT and Social Anxiety

American Psychiatric Association. (2000). *Diagnostic and statistical manual of mental disorders* (4th ed., text rev.). Washington, DC: Author.

Andrews, G., Creamer, M., Crino, R., Hunt, C., Lampe, L., & Page, A. (2003). *The treatment of anxiety disorders: Clinician guides and patient manuals* (2nd ed.). New York, NY: Cambridge University Press.

Bailey, C., & Kendel, E. (1993). Structural changes accompany memory storage. *Annual Review of Physiology. 55*, 397-426.

Barlow, D. (2002). Anxiety and its disorders: the nature and treatment of anxiety and panic (2nd ed.). New York, NY: Guilford Press.

Beck, S. (2011). *Cognitive therapy: basic and beyond* (2nd ed.).New York, NY: The Guilford Press.

Burton, L., Western, D., & Kowlalski, R. (2012). *Psychology - 3rd Australian and New Zealand Edition.* (3rd ed.). Brisbane, Australia: John Wiley & Sons.

Cannon, W. B., (1915). *Bodily changes in pain, hunger, fear and rage. (2nd ed.).* New York: Appleton-Century-Crofts. Retrieved from http://ia700408.us.archive.org/7/items/cu31924022542470/cu31924022542470.pdf

Carey, T.A., & Mullan, R. J. (2004). What is Socratic questioning?, *Psychotherapy: theory, research, practice and training, 41,* 217-226.

Choy, Y., Fyer, A.J., & Lipsitz, J. D. (2007). Treatment of specific phobia in adults. *Clinical Psychology Review, 27,* 266-286.

Clark, D. M., & Wells, A. (1995) A cognitive model of social phobia. In R.G. Heimberg, M.R. Liebowitz, D.A. Hope; and F.R. Schneider (Eds.), *Social Phobia* (pp. 69 -93). New York, NY: The Guildford Press.

Clark, M. (1999). Anxiety disorder: why they persist and how to treat them. *Behaviour research and therapy 37,* S5-S27. Retrieved from http://homepage.psy.utexas.edu/homepage/class/psy394U/Bower/12%20Anxiety%20Disorders%20/Clark-anx%20disord.pdf

Clark, M. (2001). A cognitive perspective on social phobia. In W.R. Crozier & L.E. Alden (Eds.), *International handbook on asocial anxiety: concepts, research and interventions relating to the self and shyness* (pp. 405-430). John Wiley and Sons. Retrieved from http://www.homepage.psy.utexas.edu/HomePage/Class/Psy394U/B

ower/12%20Anxiety%20Disorders%20/CLARK-SOCIAL%20PHOBIA.pdf

Coles, M.E., Hart, T.A., & Humberg, R.G (2001). Cognitive behavioral group treatment for social phobia. In Crozier, W.R., and Alden, L.E. (Eds.), *International handbook of social anxiety: concepts, research and interventions relating to self and shyness* (pp.449-470). London, UK: John Wiley and Sons Ltd.

Cooper, M. (2008). *Essential research findings in counseling and psychotherapy: the facts are friendly,* London: Sage.

Corey, G. (2011) *Theory and practice of counseling and psychotherapy, student manual.* USA: Wadsworth Publishings Co. Inc.

Doidge, N. (2010). *The brain that changes itself.* (Rev. ed.). Victoria, Australia: Scribe Publications, Pty Ltd.

Douglas S. (2001). Comorbid major depression and social phobia. *Primary Care Companion Journal of Clinical Psychiatry: Psychotherapy Casebook, 3*(4), 179-180.

Dweck, C.S (2006) *Mindset: the new psychology of success.* Random House, New York.

Freeman, A., Pretzer, j., Fleming, B., & Simon, K. M. (1990). *Clinical application of cognitive therapy.* New York: Plenum Press.

Furmark, T. (2000). *Social phobia: from epidemiology to brain function.* [Doctoral dissertation, University of Upsala] Retrieved from http://uu.diva-portal.org/smash/record.jsf?pid=diva2:166039

Grieger, R. & Boyd, J. (1980) *Rational-emotive-therapy: a skills-based approach.* New York: Van Nostrand Reinhold.

Heimberg, R. G., Liebowitz, M. R., Hope, D. A., Schneier, F. R., Holt, C. S., Welcowitz, L. A., Juster, H. R., Campeas, R., Bruch, M. A., Cloitre, M., Fallon, B., & Klein, D. F. (1998). (Cognitive behavioral group therapy vs phenelzine therapy for social phobia. *Arch Gen Psychiatry, 55(12), 1133-1141. doi:10.1001*

Heimberg, R. G., Stein, M, B., Hiripi, E., & Kessler. R. C. (2000) Trends in the prevalence of social phobia in the United States: a synthetic cohort analysis of changes over four decades. *Eur Psychiatry*, 15, 29-37.

Hoffman, S. (2008). Cognitive processes during fear acquisition and extinction in animals and humans. *Clinical Psychology Review, 28*(2), 199-210. doi:10.1016/j.cpr.2007.04.009

Holmes, J. (1993). *Between art and science: essay in psychotherapy and psychiatry.* New York, USA: Routledge.

Hope, D.A., Burns, J.A., Hyes, S.A., Herbert, J.D. & Warner, M.D. (2010). Automatic thoughts and cognitive restructuring in cognitive behavioral group therapy for social anxiety disorder. *Cognitive Therapy Research*, 34, 1-12.

Martin, G & Pear, J. (20XX). *Behaviour modification what it is and how it works*. Boston, MA: Pearson Educational International.

Neenan, M., & Dyden, W. (2011). *Rational emotive behavioral therapy in a nutshell*. (2nd ed.). London: Sage Publications.

Page, A. C., Menzies, R. G., Bryant, R. A., & Abbott, M. (2011). Anxiety disorders (pp. 45-90). In E. Rieger (Ed.), *Abnormal psychology: Leading researcher perspectives*. (2nd ed). Melbourne: McGraw-Hill.

Pull, C. B. (2005).Current status of virtual reality exposure therapy in anxiety disorder. Editorial review. *Current Opinion in Psychiatry*, 18, 7-14.

Rieger, E. (2011). *Abnormal psychology: Leading researcher perspectives*. (2nd ed.). Melbourne, Australia: McGraw-Hill.

Rogers, C. (1957).The necessary and sufficient conditions for therapeutic personality change. *Journal of consulting psychology*, 21(2), 95-103

Stein M. B., & Stein D. J. (2008). Social anxiety disorder. *Lancet*. 29, 1115-25.

Taylor, S. E., Klein, L C., Lewis, B. P., Gruenewald, T. L., Gurung, R. A., & Updgegraph, J. A. (2000). Biobehavioural responses to stress in females: tend and befriend, not fight or flight. *Psychological review*, 107, 411- 429

Tuggart, A. (2011). *A critique of CBT- part 1*. Retrieved from http://andrewjtaggart.com/2011/10/26/a-critique-of-cbt-part-1/

Watt, M., C, & DiFrancescantonio, S. (2010). Childhood Learning Experiences in the Development and Maintenance of Anxiety Disorders. Retrieved from: http://www.anxietybc.com/learning-and-anxiety

Whitfield, C. L. (2010). Psychotic drugs as agents of trauma. *The international journal of risk and safety in medicine*, 22(4), 197-207.

Article and Website

http://metapsychology.mentalhelp.net/poc/view_doc.php?type=book&id=5830

And below there is an interesting article
http://soultherapynow.com/articles/cbt-effectiveness3.html

References for Antipsychotic and Antidepressants Drugs Essay

American Psychiatric Association. *Let's talk about psychiatric drugs.* Washington, DC: American Psychiatric Association, 1993.

Back, A, T. (1972). *Depression: Causes and treatment*: Philadelphia: University of Pennsylvania Press.

Buelow, G., and Hebert, S. (1995). *Resource on psychiatric medications, issues of treatment and referral.* Pacific Grove, CA: Brooks/Cole,.

Campbell, A (2003). *An investigation into the theory of escapist behaviour and the relationship between the internet and depression, anxiety and social phobias.* The University of Sydney.

Class, S. (December 2, 2002). "Pharma Overview". http://pubs.acs.org/cen/coverstory/8048/8048pharmaceutical.html. Retrieved 2009-06-15.

Corry, M. and Tubridy, A. (2001). *Going MAD?* Newleaf publishers, Gill and Macmillan Ltd, Dublin.

Cronin Fisk, M. (2007). AstraZeneca Faces 10,000 Lawsuits Over Seroquel Drug, Bloomberg Press Retrieved from http://www.bloomberg.com/apps/news?pid=20601102&sid=a.ZT dmV67chI&refer=uk On the 16-1-2009 at 8.59 AM.

Croucher, J. "Quickstart". In *The Age Newspaper*, Melbourne, Australia, December 2003.

Davidson, R.J., & Slagter, H.A. (2000). Probing emotions in the developing brain: Functional neuroimaging in the assessment of the neural substances of emotions in normal and disordered children and adolescents. *Mental Retardation and Developmental Disabilities Research Review, 6, 3*, 166-70.

Dobbs, D.. (2006). A depression switch? *New York Times Magazine*, http://www.nytimes.com/2006/04/02/magazine/02depression

Etkin, A. & Wager, T.D. (2007). Functional neuroimaging of anxiety: A meta-analysis of emotional processing in PTSD, social anxiety disorder, and specific phobia. *American Journal of Psychiatry, 164, 10*, 1476-1488.

Eysenck, H. J. (1952). The effects of psychotherapy: An evaluation. *Journal of Cousulting Psychology, 16*, 319-324.

Main, M (1995). Attachment: overview with implication for clinical work, in S.Goldberg, R. Muir, & J. Kerr (Eds). *Attachment theory: Social developmental and clinical perspectives* (pp. 407-474). Hillsdale, NJ: Analytic Press

McGowan P., Sasaki A., D'Alessio A., Dymov S., Labonté B., Szyf M., Turecki G., Meaney M. Epigenetic regulation of the glucocorticoid receptor in human brain associates with childhood abuse. *Nat Neurosci.* 2009 February 22 12(3):342-348.

Miller, G. (2005). New neurons strive to fit in. *Science*, 311, 938-940.

Grof, S. (1976). *Realms of the Human Unconscious*. New York: Harper & Row.

Hickie, I., Davenport, T., Scott, E. (2000) Depression: out of the shadows. *The Australian women's weekly health series.*

Laing, R.D. (1982). *The Voice of Experience*. New York: Pantheon.

Martin, R, Lancet, R. (2009). *Second generation vs first generation anti psychotic drugs for schizophrenia: a meta analysis* Jan 3;373(9657):31-41. Epub 2008 Dec 6. Retrieved from http://www.ncbi.nlm.nih.gov/pubmed/19058842 on the 16-1-2009 at 12.55 PM.

McKay, K. M., Zac, E.I., & Wampold, B. E. (2006), Psychiatrist effects in the psychopharmacological treatment of depression, *Journal of Affective Disorders*, 92, 2/3, 287-290.

Messman, T. (2005). Psychiatric Drugs: Chemical Warfare on Humans: interview with Robert Whitakar retrieved from http://www.naturalnews.com/011353.html 12-1-2009.

Rizzoli, G. (2008*). Mirrors in the brain: How our mind share action and emotion.* New York: Oxford University Press.

Sapolsky, R. (1996). Why stress is bad for your brain, *Science*, 273, 749-750.

Spauwen J, Krabbendam L, Lieb R, Wittchen HU, van Os J. Impact of psychological trauma on the development of psychotic symptoms: relationship with psychosis proneness. *Br J Psychiatry.* 2006 Jun;188:527-33 Retrieved from http://www.schizophreniaforum.org/new/detail.asp?id=1271 on the 15-1-2009 at 1.42 AM.

Szasz, T. (1961). *The myth of mental illness: foundations of a theory of personal conduct*. Harper & Row.

Whitfield, L., Psychiatric Drugs as Agents of Trauma Excerpted from: *The International Journal of Risk Factor & Safety* in Medicine 22 (2010) 195- 207 DOI 10.3233/185-2010-0508.

References

Alvin, J. (1966) *Music Therapy* John Baker, Pall Mall, London.

BBC NEWS 2009 *Donor, organ "personality" worry* retrieved from http://news.bbc.co.uk/2/hi/8084936.stm on the 12th of October 2009 at 4.59 AM.

Bellecci, P.M., MD "The Heart Remembers" 2002 *The Natural Connection*. 12 November 2002 www.thenaturalconnection.net

Berger, S 2000 *Gifted Children and Sensitivity* Council for Exceptional Children retrieved from http://school.familyeducation.com/gifted-education/social-skills/38658.html on the 11th of October 2009 at 4.07 AM.

Capra, F 1983 *The Turning Point* Harper Collins Publishers, Hammersmith, London.

Capra, F., 1989 *Uncommon Wisdom,* Harper Collins Publishers, Hammersmith, London.

Carta, R., 1998 *Mapping the Mind* , Weidenfeld & Nicolson, London.

Copeland, J. in *Mindshock: Transplant Memories* source: *Mindshock: Transplanting Memories?* Channel 4 television, UK, 26 June, 2006). http://underdogcinema.com/sciencetechnology/mindshock-transplanting-memories on the 13th of October 2009.

Descares, R., in Thomas Steel Hole 197) *Tratise of Man* , Cambridge text, Cambridge.

Eales, C 1983 *Raising Your Talented Child,* Angus & Robertson Publishers, London, Sydney, Melbourne.

Freire, P 1970 *Pedagogy of the Oppressed*. New York: Herder and Herder.

Gregory, RL and Zangwill, OL 1987 *The Oxford Companion to the Mind*, New York, Oxford University Press.

Institute of Heartmath
http://www.heartmath.org/research/research-overview.html
retrieved on the 22-09-2009.

Jamison, Kay Redfield 1993 Touched with Fire: Manic-Depressive Illness and the Artistic Temperament, New York, The Free Press.

Holt, J. (1980) *The Plowboy Interview* retrieved from http://www.motherearthnews.com/Nature-Community/1980-07-01/Plowboy-Interview-John-Holt.aspx?page=5 on the 10th of October 2009 at 6.51 AM.

Illich, I. (1972) Interview conducted in Cuernavaca, Mexico, at the Center for Intercultural Documentation (CIdoc), transcript available from the Network for Cultural Alternatives, 477 Fourteenth Street, Brooklyn, N.Y. 11215.

Laing, R. (1967) *The Politics of Experience* London: Penguin Books.

McCraty, R., Atkinson, M., Bradley,RT., The Journal of Alternative and Complementary Medicine. February 2004, 10(1): 133-143. doi:10.1089/107555304322849057. Published in Volume: 10 Issue 1: June 30, 2004 retrieved from http://www.liebertonline.com/doi/abs/10.1089/107555304322849 057?cookieSet=1&journalCode=acm on the 12th of October 2009.

New Scientist magazine, issue 2526, 19 November 2005, page 20.

Peterson JB, Smith KW, Caron S 2002 Openness and extraversion are associated with reduced latent inhibition: replication and commentary. Personality and Individual Differences 33(7):1137-1147.

Picasso, P. (1937) *Abstract Expressionism Master Bill* American Artists Congress. Retrieved from http://www.warholstars.org/abstractexpressionism/timeline/abstra ctexpressionism37.html On the 9th of October 2009.

Post, F. (1996), Verbal creativity, depression and alcoholism: an investigation of one hundred American and British writers. *Br J Psychiatry* 168(5):545-555

Salem, M. (2007) The Heart, Mind and Spirit retrieved from http://www.rcpsych.ac.uk/pdf/Heart,%20Mind%20and%20Spirit %20%20Mohamed%20Salem.pdf on the 12th October 2009

Samuel, G., (1990) *Mind, Body and Culture* (1990) Cambridge University Press, Cambridge, New York, Port Chester, Melbourne, Sydney.

Szabolcs K-ri (2009) Research study examines the link between neuregulin 1 and creativity retrieved from http://www.news-medical.net/news/20090929/Research-study-examines-the-link-between-neuregulin-1-gene-and-creativity.aspx on the 11th of October 2009

Simonton, D, (2004) *Ceativity in science: chance, logic, genius, and zeitgeist.* New York: Cambridge University Press.

Wertheim, M., Alas Poor Zombie. Cosmos. October/November 2006. Published in Volume: 001 issue 11.

Zorah, D. and Marshall, I. (2000) *Spiritual IQ* Sunday Telegraph the Sunday Magazine. August 6, 20-22.

Index

A

Abilify, 118
ADD, 79
Adderall, 118
ADHD, 111
Agitated Depression, 23
alcohol, 18, 50
alcoholism, 37, 99, 161, 167, 168
    of father, 47
Alvin, J., 48
Anti Stigma Crusaders Journal, 3, 52
anticonvulsant, 24, 63
antidepressants, 23, 35, 41, 62, 63, 111,
    114–18, 117, 118, 146, 157
    and hypomania, 49
anti-psychotics, 105, 114
artist
    meaning of, 49
AstraZeneca, 112, 113, 181
Attention Deficit Disorder. *See* ADD
Australia, 78, 80

B

biomedical model, 77, 79
Bipolar Disorder
    and childhood trauma, 16
Bipolar I
    and Cheryl, 54
    defined, 15
Bipolar II
    defined, 5
    diagnosis, 29
    stigma, 28
Bipolar Light, 29
Borderline Personality Disorder. *See*
    BPD

BPD, 15, 101
burning, 17–18, 30
Butler, 29, 40, 55

C

Canetti, E., 75–76
capitalism, 64, 66, 69, 70, 71
Cavanagh, D., 55
CBT, 18, 24, 78, 87, 89–96
    and pharmacotherapy, 95
    defined, 94
    homework, 95
childhood trauma, 11–16
Cock, P., 75
Cognitive Behavioral Therapy. *See* CBT
Copeland, J., 154
Corcoran, P., 55, 78
Corry, M., 7
creativity, 121–49
    and mindfulness, 140–41
    defined, 122
Croucher, J.S., 118
Csikszentmihalyi, M., 132
cyclothymia, 29, 108, 119, 137

D

Dabrowski, K., 144
darwinism, social, 67–68
Dawkins, R., 67, 73
depression
    and spirituality, 62
    controlling, 167
    unipolar, 140
    vegetative, 24
Doidge, 86, 94, 175
dopamine, 114
Dreyfuss, R., 4

Drug-Stress Trauma Syndrome, 119
drunk driving, 23

E

Eales, C., 125
Effexor, 115, 116, 117, 118
Eli Lilly, 112
Epilim, 24, 29, 63
Eysenck, H.J., 86, 111

F

Fluoxetine, 112
Freire, P., 4, 6, 124
Fry, S., 29, 119, 137

H

hallucinations, 114
Harris, T., 5
HeartMath, 155–56
Holt, J., 95, 124, 179
homelessness, 3, 20–21
Hood, B., 154
humanistic psychology, 7, 18
hypomania
    uncontrolled, 29

I

Imipramine, 118
Intrinsic Cardiac Ganglia, 152–53
IQ, 68, 127, 144

J

Jamison, K., 138

K

Kaczynski, T., 144
Klonopin, 118
Kropotkin, P., 73

L

Lamictal, 118
Lautrec, H., 159–66
Leahy, T., 69
Lexapro, 117
liberalism, 65–66

Lithium, 63

M

Major Depression, 5, 6, 15, 28, 79, 90,
    104, 111, 179
marijuana, 23, 50
Marx, 68–72
Maslow, A., 18
Matè, G., 98
McCarty, R., 155–56
Mellaril, 54
mental illness
    and childhood trauma, 11–16, 97–
        105
    and creativity, 136
    and social status, 56
    as personality, 170
Mill, S., 72–73
mindfulness, 29, 63, 119, 140–41, 142,
    151
Moulin Rouge, 162–64
music therapy, 47–48

N

neglect, 101
neuregulin 1, 136, 137
neuroleptic state, 114
NRG1. *See* neuregulin 1

O

Obsessive Compulsive Disorder. *See*
    OCD
OCD, 30

P

Pax Medica, 79, 111
    defined, 77
person-centered, 78, 85
Picasso, 125, 126, 127, 130, 135, 141,
    163, 165
placebo, 41, 49, 114, 115, 117, 118
Post Traumatic Stress Disorder. *See*
    PTSD
protestantism, 66–67
Prozac. *See* Fluoxetine
psychology
    as science, 81

psychosis, 11, 15, 16, 37, 38, 39, 62,
   118, 136, 137
   and childhood trauma, 101–4
psychotropic medications, 86, 101, 111
PTSD, 13, 21, 91, 101, 103, 104, 181

R

rational intelligence, 127
resilience, 7, 50, 97, 98, 100
Rich, R., v–vi, 11, 22–23, 41, 55, 82, 86,
   99, 108, 114
Rogers, C., 7, 9, 18, 78
Rozelle Hospital, 4, 30, 37, 39, 40, 43,
   44, 48, 49, 50
Ruse, M., 67, 68

S

Salem, M.O., 151–52, 157
schizophrenia
   and childhood trauma, 15
   and psychologists, 79
   misdiagnosis of, 54
Scientology, 15
selective serotonin reuptake. *See* SSRI
self-harm, 17–18, 30, 33, 35
   reasons, 33
self-sabotage, 23
Seroquel, 112, 113, 118, 181
shoplifting, 23
Shumann, R., 139
Singer, P., 73–74
Skinner, 78, 85, 86, 93
Smith, A., 72–73
Spencer, H., 66–67
spirituality, 61–64
SSRI, 112, 116, 117

St. Vincent's Hospital, 50, 54
Stella
   about, 4–5, 56
stigma, 64
substance abuse, 102
Sydney, 4, 20, 49, 164, 181, 183, 184

T

tardive dyskinesia, 113
TAUTOA, 97, 98, 99
Terrigal, NSW, 47
Tubridy, A., 7, 98, 101, 181

U

Unabomber, 144

V

van Gogh, 4, 123, 136, 162, 163
vegetative depression, 24
vicious circle, 20

W

Waring, T., 3, 55
Whitaker, R., 118
Wilks, C., 85
World Trade Center, 127

Y

Yorke, T., 158

Z

Zotti, Cheryl, 49, 52–54

Beyond Schizophrenia: Michael's Journey

What would you do if your child suffered with something so severe it affected every aspect of his life?

Susie Dunham, Midwestern mom and former nurse, never suspected her son Michael was anything but a typical college student with big dreams until he developed schizophrenia shortly after his 21st birthday.

The Dunham family quickly becomes immersed in the nightmare world of mental illness in America: psychiatric wards, a seemingly indifferent nursing staff, and the trial-and-error world of psychotropic meds. Michael's ultimate recovery and remission comes with plenty of traumatic incidents involving both ignorance and stigma, but his courage and quest for dignity will inspire all readers.

"Susie Dunham's heroic, heart-rending story is a beacon of light in the darkness of insanity. It shows that recovery is hard-won but possible for people who develop schizophrenia, despite a media that sensationalizes them, a society that shuns them, and a dysfunctional mental healthcare system that fails them miserably."

--Patrick Tracey, author of *Stalking Irish Madness: Searching for the Roots of My Family's Schizophrenia*

"*Beyond Schizophrenia: Michael's Journey* is a book that I couldn't put down. The story of Michael's parents Susie and Mark who support their son both in good times and bad really touched me. I really like the way the symptoms of schizophrenia are explained clearly."

--Bill MacPhee, Founder/CEO of SZ Magazine

Available in trade paperback and eBook editions
ISBN 978-1-61599-035-1
Learn more at **www.SusieDunham.org**

Holli Kenley's *Mountain Air* helps your personal journey!

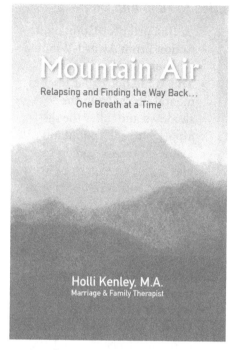

Deep down inside, each of us knows what our truths are.

It is forgivable to lose them... it is unforgivable not to re-claim them...

Mountain Air: Relapsing And Finding The Way Back One Breath At A Time is a brutally honest personal narrative detailing a painful decent into relapse and a powerful journey back to recovering.

Without condemnation but with passion and purpose, *Mountain Air* ...

- Embraces individuals who have abandoned their authentic ways of being for a life of personal neglect, indulgence, or self-destruction.
- Speaks to individuals who have betrayed their healing tenets - the addict who has lost his sobriety, the abused who has returned to her abuser, or the codependent who continues to rescue the uncontrollable.
- Reaches out to individuals who have maintained a life of stability and wellness, but who are eroding over time – and losing their sense of self and of spirit.

Mountain Air is for any individual who has experienced relapse and who is fighting to find his way back...

- By inviting readers to take a journey with the author as she shares time-tested lessons in the recovering process.
- By providing thoughtful and accountable exercises with each chapter that guide the reader in the reclaiming and sustaining of their truths.

"This poetic and nature-infused account should become a standard for all therapists and all in the process of recovery."

--David Van Nuys, Ph.D, Host of Shrink Rap Radio

ISBN 978-1-932690-76-7

Learn more at **www.HolliKenley**

CPSIA information can be obtained
at www.ICGtesting.com
Printed in the USA
LVHW080714241118
598012LV00018B/617/P